Christian Symbols, Ancient Roots

of related interest

Dramatherapy with Families, Groups and Individuals
Waiting in the Wings
Sue Jennings
1990 ISBN 1 85302 048 6 hb, 1992 ISBN 1 85302 144 X pb

Drama and Healing
The Roots of Drama Therapy
Roger Grainger
1990 ISBN 1 85302 048 6

Art Therapy and Dramatherapy
Masks of the Soul
Sue Jennings & Ase Minde
1992 ISBN 1 85302 027 3

Storymaking in Education and Therapy
Alida Gersie & Nancy King
1990 ISBN 1 85302 519 4 hb, ISBN 1 85302 520 8 pb

Storymaking in Bereavement
Dragons Fight in the Meadow
Alida Gersie
1991 ISBN 1 85302 065 6 hb, 1992 ISBN 1 85302 176 8 pb

Playtherapy with Abused Children
Ann Cattanach
1992 ISBN 1 85302 120 2

Symbols of the Soul
Therapy and Guidance Through Fairy Tales
Birgitte Brun, Ernst W Pedersen & Marianne Runberg
1992 ISBN 1 85302 107 5

Focus on Psychodrama
The Therapeutic Aspects of Psychodrama
Peter Felix Kellermann
1992 ISBN 1 85302 127 X

The Metaphoric Body
A Guide to Expressive Therapy Through Images and Archetypes
Leah Bartal & Nira Ne'eman
1993 ISBN 1 85302 152 X

Christian Symbols, Ancient Roots

Elizabeth Rees

Jessica Kingsley Publishers
London & Philadelphia

First published in the United Kingdom in 1992 by
Jessica Kingsley Publishers Ltd
116 Pentonville Road
London N1 9JB

Copyright © 1992 Elizabeth Rees

British Library Cataloguing in Publication Data
Rees, Elizabeth
    Christian Symbols, Ancient Roots
    I. Title
    246

ISBN 1 85302 046 X

Printed and Bound in Great Britain by
Biddles Ltd., Guildford and King's Lynn

Contents

Illustrations

Acknowledgements

I should like to thank the people who helped this book to emerge. First my parents, who took their four children off to explore Roman villas, Celtic saints' dwellings and medieval churches, until I felt a part of my history. Next my Oxford college tutor, David Wulstan, who showed me that music was rooted in magic. Thirdly, the artist Meinrad Craighead who taught me how to celebrate creation in symbol and worship as we shared four years of monastic life. Then Sr. Giotto Moots, whose Centre for Sacred Arts in New Mexico was a source of life and learning in the 1970s, and whose lectures on Christian Iconography were for me a key to unlock medieval thought and prayer.

In my collaboration with Dr. Sue Jennings over the last five years I have learnt to place my Christian story in an anthropological context; she has given bones and sinews to my Christian vision. Dom Gregory van der Kleij helped me to grasp aspects of violence and healing within Christian worship, and Dr. Hélène La Rue clarified my ideas about shamans. Margaret Rees has made many helpful suggestions about the text of this book, and with a photographer's knack of being in the right place at the right time, she has provided plates which illustrate people at work symbol-making. Steven Nemethy has kindly drawn many of the figures.

Finally, I thank the sisters of Turvey Abbey who have opened their monastery to me for five summers now, enabling me to bring students so we can come to grips with Christian symbols in life and in worship. Benedictines spend as much time making ritual as they do sleeping or eating, but few communities are as willing as Turvey is to share their hearth and their sacred space with all who come.

Elizabeth Rees

Foreword

It is with great pleasure that I am writing the foreword to Elizabeth Rees's very special book. It has grown out of extensive research, discussion and exploration in a field which straddles several disciplines—the arts, theology, social anthropology, and folklore.

The author and I first discussed the idea of this book during an Arts and Liturgy Summer School at Turvey Abbey in Bedfordshire. Liz organised the whole school and led a musical composition class, Sr. Esther taught sacred art through icon and posters, and I conducted a group on sacred dance. The participants in the dance group chose a biblical text to develop through movement and symbol. The outcome was very moving and highly creative, in a group of people with an age range from 21 to 71 years, many of whom had never been in an experimental workshop before. The elderly lady who 'grew' as the strong ears of corn amongst the tares said she felt a new person, re-vitalised with energy. The whole group dramatised through movement and sound the crossing of the Red Sea and Moses' people pursued by the Egyptians. Nuns in habit and teachers in jeans experimented with the aggressive movements of the Egyptians and the fear of the Israelites, with the Red Sea being symbolised by a large length of red material which eventually rose to cover the heads of the Egyptians. The whole scene was highly charged and brought fresh understanding of the dynamics and the importance of the symbols. The two examples described above illustrate the richness in natural symbols—the corn and the water—which were chosen spontaneously by the group. The symbols themselves made a big impact on the participants as they literally 'embodied' the symbols in the enactment. Liz and I said then that this type of material should be made more accessible to other people, whether they were therapists, teachers or theologians, in a form that would allow the reader to become involved in the text rather than dryly to analyse it. We decided to write a book jointly on the ancient roots of Christian symbols.

Since that first discussion several years ago, there have been some developments. The material has expanded into an unwieldy amount, which has made us decide to publish two books rather than one. Therefore, I am writing the foreword to this volume, written by Elizabeth Rees and she will write the foreword to the volume written by me. However, the essential themes are the same even though Liz may write from a more theological stance and I from a more anthropological perspective; we are both in complete agreement that dominant Christian symbols are rooted in ancient history and became integrated into Christianity with added meaning and values.

It is a mark of 20th century culture, and Christianity too, that the world of symbol is impoverished. This is noticeable in worship as well as in healing, where both churches and hospitals are influenced by 'high-tech'. Not that I am criticising high tech *per se*—rather mourning its replacement of ritual and symbol.

As a dramatherapist, I am acutely aware of the power of these symbols in healing—both in a preventative as well as curative sense. Ancient healing rituals in pre-Christian times as well as in the time of our Lord used dominant symbols such as water, blood, and corn. It is to the detriment of the church that many rituals were banned, the most dramatic being those of medieval wise women. The so-called witches were the wise women of the time and for the majority of people, their only source of medicine. They used substances still used in medicine today to relieve pain and fever, and performed powerful rituals at times of childbirth. The Church and state mounted a determined campaign to exterminate the wise women saying, amongst other things, that the pain of childbirth had to be endured as punishment—surely an attitude derived from Old Testament retribution rather than from Christ's own healing ministry. Ancient symbols and rituals are in themselves a remedy which I hope this book will help us rediscover once again. In this volume, the author takes the dominant symbols that occur in Christianity and traces their history through ancient myths and beliefs of many cultures. My volume will develop these ideas in healing practice, both ancient and modern. I continue to teach with Elizabeth Rees as we develop and expand our own perception of sacred arts and Christian symbolism—she is a most enriching person to be with and her creative energy challenges the most orthodox assumptions. I commend her book to you, knowing that you also will find enrichment and succour.

Sue Jennings
Stratford-upon-Avon
September 1991

CHAPTER 1

The Ancient Roots of Christian Symbols

We had almost given up our search in a remote spot of Cornwall for the twin holy wells and chapel which our map described. Finally we stumbled on them, and found pure water which had been used for drinking, healing and baptising for many centuries. Close to the wells, villagers had tied rags to the hawthorn tree, as mute prayers for healing, or thanks for good things. The chapel, water and rags are each symbols, or connections with the holy, for the people who use them, and these three symbols have been used since long before Christianity. A chapel is a sacred space whose walls mark the boundary between chaos outside and harmonious peace within. Spring water, or living water wells up from the heart of the earth, a tiny river of life. Like crutches hanging round the grotto at Lourdes, the rags at the well are personal symbols of each person who brought them, each with its silent story.

Symbols in Worship
We use a wealth of symbols in our lives, particularly in our worship. This is because symbols always point to the transcendent; they link what is human to the cosmos. In worship we are able to express the light and shadow of our lives through symbols. We ritualise our violence in the sacrifice of the Mass, bringing with us our various ways of dealing with death, as we expose ourselves to the love of God. When we enact our violence in sacred time and space, we experience integration and healing, as do the participants of a psychodrama, or an audience watching a profound play. In a penitential rite composed by a group of people to use at Mass, four 'victims' lay face downwards on the floor. Their 'oppressors' raised their fists and each planted a foot on their victim's back. The group prayed: 'For the times we have oppressed others, Lord, have mercy'. The victims then turned to their oppressors, asking to be trodden on yet again. The group prayed 'For the times we have invited others to oppress us, Christ, have mercy'. Those enacting this simple ritual linked their personal struggle with that of people in every age through the symbols they chose.

Symbols find their most natural setting in ritual. A couple symbolise their affection in a wedding ceremony. They solemnly enact their commitment, exchanging rings and promises. We symbolise our grief at a funeral, in our particular culture, through sombre clothes and music, through mourners and flowers. Ritual centres and energises us. The second century 'Acts of John' describes Jesus after the Last Supper performing a ritualised circle dance with his disciples. Fra Angelico portrayed angels inviting saints into the heavenly round dance, while Botticelli tells us that heaven is wedded to earth at the nativity of Christ by painting angels performing a circle dance above the stable at Bethlehem.

Medieval artists spoke in symbols, sharing their faith through their work. On church walls where the paintwork survives, St. Michael portrays our struggle against evil as he triumphantly slays Satan, and St. Christopher, the giant who supposedly carried the Christ child across a raging torrent, reminds us that we will be carried safely across the troubled waters of life. Today, artists, sculptors and embroiderers search for symbols both old and new in order to speak words of life to their worshipping community. Symbols enrich our understanding; symbolism adds value to an object or act, and makes it more powerful. Through symbolism we can turn an object or an action into an open event, and can open the door on to immediate reality. In this way our universe is no longer fragmented or sealed off. Through symbols we can grasp reality.

Symbol for Ancient Peoples

We can trace the beginnings of symbolic thought back to prehistoric times, to the late palaeolithic period. We can tell from their belongings and their art, especially their engravings, how these people approached the invisible world through visible symbols: the constellations, plants and animals, rocks and stones. Late neolithic peoples gave a new importance to the sun and moon and to sacred stones, and conceived of space in geometric terms. All these symbols are used in monuments such as Stonehenge.

The new development of agriculture in Egypt and the near east before 3000 BC led to the appreciation of further symbols. By growing crops, people came to appreciate the annual rhythm of growth, flowering and coming to fruit, and of sowing and harvesting. This rhythm was related to the calendar, which was calculated from the positions of the heavenly bodies. Megalithic culture developed commemorative stones and giant sacred buildings with their pillars and lintels. They evolved other powerful symbols: eye-shaped ornaments, family trees, signal drums, death ships and labyrinths. They invented rituals: head hunting and the sacrifice of oxen. Megalithic culture has given us our most powerful symbols.

The people of ancient Egypt developed a new awareness of the relation between the material and spiritual worlds, as we can tell from their religion and from their hieroglyphic writings. In Egypt, a study of the planets led people to experience them as aspects of God, or deities. This concept was further developed in ancient Greece and Rome, whose peoples gave us, for example, Apollo, Jupiter, Ceres and Mars. Their stories are vivid and dramatic, expressed in art, myth, legend and poetry. For ancient Egyptians, Greeks and Romans, worship was colourful and powerful.

Symbol and Emotion

In our culture we have considerably narrowed down our way of worship; mostly we worship with our brains. At Mass, when I sit alongside someone in the process of becoming a Catholic and explain in whispers what is going on, I sense their bewilderment. We bring our hearts along, but the language we speak is too intellectual. Symbolism is a language of images and emotions. It is also a dynamic and dramatic language, because it can express simultaneously the various aspects or opposites of the idea it represents. The worshippers who devised the penitential rite became both victims and oppressors, to symbolise both sides of oppression. They expressed the weakness and strength which we all know from experience. By integrating both these polarities, we become whole.

Symbols teach us about who we are. They are lamps with which we can explore our inner world. Christian theologians have not until recently shown great respect for the human psyche. They have been more concerned with teaching timeless truths to erring humanity. Christian theologians have held God in such reverence that human beings have generally emerged as second class. Previous cultures did not fall so far into this trap. In most ancient cultures you could become a hero, if at times a tragic one.

Symbols Become Fossilised

Symbols also lead us into the world of psychology, for symbols live in our psyche. Psychology, or the science of the human mind, is a relatively new discipline, and Christian theologians have, by and large, been reluctant to explore the immense horizons which psychology has opened up concerning the mystery and depths of the human person. Vatican documents on behavioural issues typically dismiss the findings of psychology as self-centred and humanistic. In doing so they risk denying the central Christian truth, that God became human. Recent theologies, however, instead of condemning humanistic self-centredness, focus on the value of human self-centring, and Christian thinkers are gradually becoming less hesitant to situate their theology within a broader psychological perspective.

Holy things and actions easily become fossilised, especially when they are handed down through many centuries, and their roots are forgotten. The average Catholic, if asked about holy things and actions, will talk about the seven sacraments which Jesus instituted. Medieval theologians taught this too; they did not know that Jesus created no new rituals at all, or that a meal of bread and wine was a religious practice centuries before the time of Jesus. Only in the mid-twelfth century did theologians evolve a definition of a sacrament, and decide that seven rituals fitted the categories which they defined; and since seven was a number which symbolised wholeness, they were happy with their decision. From that time onwards, Christians have tended to separate off their particular holy things and actions from the rest of life. As a result, Christian holy things have become too magical and too little integrated with the rich world of symbols that surrounds us.

An Earlier, Broader Vision

If we examine Christian traditions before the middle ages, we find a more creative interplay between theology and the surrounding world. For St. Augustine, in the fifth century, sacraments and symbols were fairly interchangeable concepts. Augustine described sacraments as 'visible forms of invisible grace', and included a wide variety of actions and objects in his list: the kiss of peace, the font of baptism, blessed salt, the creed, the Our Father, the ashes of penance. Thinking more broadly still, he wrote: 'All organic and inorganic things in nature bear spiritual messages through their distinctive forms and characteristics'. Augustine valued all these symbols because they awaken our energy and love: 'Teaching carried out with the help of symbols feeds and stirs the fires of love' (Augustine of Hippo 1930, *Letter 55*).

Early Christians knew that many of their rituals were very old. St. Paul explained to the Greek Christians in Corinth that the ancient Israelites experienced the sacraments as did the new Christians. The Israelite slaves who escaped from Egypt were all baptised by their passage through the Red Sea as they passed from death into new life, and just as the Corinthians shared bread and wine in their Christian Eucharist, so the Israelites in the desert all shared manna, or bread from heaven, and drank from the spiritual rock that followed them (1 *Corinthians*. 10:1–4).

Sacraments are Symbols

Theologians explain sacraments as outer signs of inner realities, and that is a fair definition of a symbol. Unlike abstract ideas, symbols bring us into touch with realities which are both familiar and mysterious. A symbol leads us into the mystery which it stands for, and all true symbols affect us. When a loving couple notice and feel their wedding rings during the day, they remember their love for each other, and deepen it too. The wedding rings express eternal love: a holy thing. Most symbols are religious images; they point to the transcendent. Symbols come from a very deep level of our awareness, and have been with us for many thousands of years. They help us to value objects and acts by pointing to the deep reality they contain. They link human experience to the cosmos, and they help us to order our world.

Symbolism is a language not of abstractions but of feelings and images. In Christianity the symbol of the cross, for example, expresses a multitude of ideas and emotions. A third century poem describes the cross as the tree of life which grows to an immense height and stretches out its arms, gathering the whole world in its grasp; at its foot the baptismal spring bubbles forth, and all nations hurry to the spot to drink everlasting life. The poem ends:

> Thence we go to heaven by way of the branches of the high tree. This is the wood of life to all that believe. Amen.

> (Pseudo-Cyprian in Rahner (i) 1963, p.52)

Preaching to candidates for baptism on the site of Calvary a hundred years later, Bishop Cyril of Jerusalem used powerful symbolic language to describe the cross as the centre of the universe, around which the world turns: 'God stretched forth his hands upon the cross in order to embrace the utmost limits of the earth, and this makes the hill of Golgotha the pivot of the world' (Cyril of Jerusalem in Rahner (i) 1963, p.52).

We are all symbol-producing individuals, and the history of symbolism shows that everything can assume symbolic significance: natural objects (such as trees, stones, mountains, sun and moon, fire and water), human artefacts (such as wedding rings, the cross, the hearth, the ark of safety) and even abstract forms such as numbers, the square and the circle. As St. Paul said, through visible things we learn to appreciate invisible ones, and all of us can touch God in this way (Romans 1:20). When we transform objects into symbols, we give them great psychological power; we then express them in our worship and in our art. From prehistoric times onwards, the intertwined history of religion and art records the symbols that have moved people and given meaning to their lives.

Archetypes

When we are alert to symbols, we are attentive to the meaning of life. Jung observed that most of his patients were people who had lost their faith, and who as a result had no church to help them make sense of symbols. Today, the same is true for most churchgoers too—we possess few meaningful images to shape our lives, and are forced to express our faith in bland and colourless ways. Yet symbols are always with us, acting on us before we realise what is happening. We are surrounded by the symbols and stories of our family and our society from the time of our birth. Before we know how to reflect, we begin to discover the richness of what 'father' and 'mother' mean. These are emotion-charged images found in almost every culture. For the American Indians, Mother Earth and Father Sky nourish and give life to their countless children. For ourselves, mother earth, mother Church and mother Mary contain a wealth of elements of which we are largely unconscious, both nurturing and threatening, which affect us throughout our lives. Similarly, the concept of father has been powerful in most cultures, from the Israelite warrior God who killed Egyptian babies to the loving father of Jesus's parable who ran out to embrace his prodigal son.

Jung described such emotion-charged images as archetypes. He thought of archetypes as dynamic nuclei of the psyche, which have an enormous impact on us, forming our emotions and outlook, and influencing our relationships with others. Archetypal images affect people differently. The cross, for example, may mean little to a non-Christian, while for a Christian it gains psychic energy and takes on life. Archetypes are creative and can inspire new ideas, but they can be destructive too if these ideas stiffen into prejudices which inhibit further discovery. Such prejudice can lead to bitter religious persecution, as history shows; but when we befriend these powerful symbols, they bring us wholeness and healing.

Hero's Journey

Religion is rich in archetypal symbols. Beside those of mother and father, that of hero is widely found. He is a leader who has dangerous adventures and opens up a way for his followers. For the ancient Greeks, Orpheus was such a hero. He was probably a real man, a singer, prophet and teacher, who was martyred and whose tomb became a shrine. Although his cult was rooted in the agricultural cycle of birth, growth, fullness and decay, early Christians saw him as a symbol of their hero Christ, since both were seen to mediate the divine in the late Hellenistic culture of the Roman empire, offering a future life to their followers. Like Christ, Orpheus was a Good Shepherd; when he sang, wild animals lay in peace at his feet, and the wind and sea became still, as they did when Christ calmed the storm and his followers asked 'What kind of man is this, that the wind and the sea obey him?' (Luke 8:25). Orpheus taught while he sang and played the lyre; he mediated devotion and harmony. He appears in Christian catacomb paintings with his lyre, surrounded by wild animals, now a figure of Christ. As a hero, Christ encountered the demons of evil, descended into hell and redeemed his people. He exemplified the struggle between good and evil, and the achievement of human potential. Other heroes are St. George and King Arthur, and we are all heroes in our own way, as we move through life's adventures.

The journey or pilgrimage is another ancient archetype. The runaway Israelite slaves journeyed for forty years through the desert towards their promised land. Throughout Christian times, countless pilgrims have journeyed to the Holy Land or to their sacred shrines, as the Canterbury Tales of Chaucer describe. The Church is a pilgrim people, on its way to life with God for ever. The theme of a lonely pilgrimage to obtain deeper life through renunciation and atonement is found in many cultures. Young American Indians of the Pacific

Northwest make a lonely pilgrimage to a crater lake where, in a trance-like state, they encounter a guardian spirit in the form of an animal, bird or natural object. The youth identifies with this 'bush soul' and thereby becomes a man. He has discovered a symbol which describes his inner life and helps him to know himself with deeper awareness. We have always used animal symbols to capture human qualities: Jesus told his followers to be wise as serpents yet gentle as doves. His followers described him as a lamb, a serpent exalted on the cross, a fish, a lion, a unicorn.

Stone Statues

Another archetypal symbol is the stone or statue. Natural stones were highly symbolic for ancient peoples. They were believed to mark the homes of gods and spirits, and were used to mark tombs, boundaries and places of prayer. The Old Testament story of Jacob's dream illustrates how stones symbolised God, and somehow connected people with God: 'At sunset Jacob came to a holy place and slept there. He lay down to sleep, resting his head on a stone. He dreamt that he saw a ladder reaching from earth to heaven, with angels going up and coming down on it. And there was the Lord standing beside him. "I am the Lord, the God of Abraham and Isaac", he said. "I will give to you and to your descendents this land on which you are lying...I will be with you and protect you wherever you go, and I will bring you back to this land..." Jacob woke up and said, "The Lord is here! He is in this place and I never knew it." He was afraid and said, "What a terrifying place this is! It must be the house of God; it must be the gate that opens into heaven". Jacob got up early next morning, took the stone that was under his head and set it up as a memorial. Then he poured olive oil on it to dedicate it to God. He named the place Bethel ("House of God")... Then Jacob made a vow to the Lord...: "This memorial stone which I have set up will be the place where you are worshipped, and I will give you a tenth of everything you give me" (*Genesis* 28:11–22).

Early in history, sculptors tried to express the spirit of a rock by giving it the hint of a human figure; many statues of the earth mother take this form. Ancient Israelites held that God was too holy to be represented in any form, but early Christians, influenced by surrounding cultures, developed a rich tradition of statues and paintings. One of the earliest forms of Christian statue was that of the *virgo lactans*, the mother of God seated, suckling her child. This beautiful image illustrates the central myth, or story, of Christianity: the incarnation, the story of God becoming human to make us divine.

Truth and Myth

Myth is not a derogatory word. Christian thinkers have generally held that myths (except for their own) were false and absurd, but in the last century we have rediscovered the value and purpose of myth. While ethnologists studying archaic societies have explored the meaning of their myths, Freud and Jung have linked the contents of ancient myths with the unconscious mind of modern men and women. Jung observed that all the energy and interest which we today devote to science and technology was devoted by ancient peoples to mythology. Myths are stories containing moral principles, laws of nature and the great transformations that take place in human life and in the life of the universe. They are treasured holy stories which tell how something came into being; how people, animals or institutions were created, or how the world or death came into being. The actors in myths are often heavenly beings who do holy work by creating something, but the myth is also a pattern or model for what people do now. A Brahman text proclaims: 'We must do what the gods did in the beginning'.

Creation Myths

Myths which describe the creation of the universe are found everywhere. The book of *Genesis* opens with two distinct creation myths. In the first, God creates light and dark, land and sea, animals and people on successive days (*Genesis* 1:1–24). In the second, God plants a garden watered by a spring, makes the first people out of dust, and puts them in the garden (*Genesis* 2:5–16). Other cultures have different myths to explain how people were created. The story of Noah's ark and the great flood found later in *Genesis* (6:2–9:17) is an example of another myth common to many cultures, telling the story of how an old world was destroyed and a new one created. In this story, God grieves because his world has grown evil. He instructs Noah to take his family and some animals into a ship which will be able to sail safely above the disastrous flood which will destroy everything. When the waters recede, Noah emerges to build a new world, and God sets a rainbow in the sky as a promise that he will not flood the earth again. Other flood stories are found in India, Burma and other parts of South East Asia; in Australia, New Zealand and New Guinea; in North and South America, and in parts of Europe.

Myths continue the story of the world's creation in some way, and help it to happen. The American Indians of Taos pueblo in New Mexico believe that their religious ceremonies help the sun to rise and set. Their chief, Mountain Lake, explained to Jung: 'We are a people who live on the roof of the world; we are sons of Father Sun, and with our religion we daily help our father to go across the sky. We do this not only for ourselves, but for the whole world. If we were to cease practising our religion, in ten years the sun would no longer rise. Then it would be night forever' (Guzie 1981, p.118).

Before scorning the magic which this ritual implies, we should remember how Catholics would speak of the priest's power to make God come down on the altar in the form of bread and wine. In fact, neither pueblo Indians nor Catholics can make God more present in this way; rather they become more present themselves to the mystery of God's life at work in the world. Both these rituals attempt to explain that we are necessary to complete God's creation: we are the second creators of the world. The greatest act of creation in which we engage is to become fully human; Christians express this in the story of the incarnation: God becoming fully human, and enabling us to do so too.

Rituals Enact Our Story

Rituals express the myths we live by. People retell the old stories in ceremonies that make the ancient acts come alive again. The Kali of New Guinea say 'It was thus that the (mythical) ancestors did, and we do the same'. In ancient Mesopotamia, the world was ritually recreated during the New Year festival. The Poem of Creation was recited in the temple, and a series of rites re-enacted the fight between Marduk (the creator god) and Tiamat (a dragon symbolising the primordial ocean of chaos). The central Christian rituals are much more intimate, since they are concerned with incarnation, with creating our humanity more fully. The symbolic rituals of the sacraments are all expressions of human intimacy: a bath, rubbing with fragrant oil, a meal of bread and wine, kissing, laying on of hands. Originally these actions were carried out lovingly by the community in a house church, although their intimacy has largely been lost over the centuries.

Another ritual common to most cultures is that of initiation. Through this rite, young men and women are weaned away from their parents and made members of their clan or tribe. The group becomes a second family, to which the young are symbolically sacrificed, to re-emerge into a new life. An example of this rite of passage through death to rebirth is circumcision, practised in many archaic cultures and by ancient Israelites and modern Jews alike. Initiation essentially begins with a rite of submission, followed by a period of containment and a further rite of liberation. Submission may involve an ordeal or trial of strength. Fasting, tattooing or a mutilation such as circumcision creates a symbolic mood of death from which rebirth comes. Early Christians struggled to decide whether circumcision was essential to their own initiation. Their arguments are described in the *Acts of the Apostles*: 'Some men came down from Judaea and taught the brothers, "Unless you have yourselves circumcised in the tradition of Moses, you cannot be saved". This led to disagreement...' After a long argument, St. Paul went to Jerusalem to discuss the problem with the other Christian leaders. They concluded that their own water baptism ritual was sufficient (*Acts* 15:1–21).

By the fourth century, baptism entailed a rite of enrolment at the beginning of Lent, followed by forty days of fasting, prayer and preparation as the community leaders taught their candidates about the great mystery they were to enter at Easter. On Easter night, death and rebirth were acted out in a ceremony in which each candidate was pushed underwater with prayer, to emerge newborn from the womb of Mother Church. They were rubbed all over with fragrant oil, clothed in new white robes, and at once shared the holy meal of bread and wine with their new family, the Christian community. Catholic theologians today are trying to restore the elements of this initiation in a programme entitled the 'Rite of Christian Initiation of Adults', in which the community prepares candidates for baptism over a period of time, and various ancient rites mark stages of this process. Contemporary theologians have drawn up this programme of initiation after rediscovering ancient Christian rituals and thinking them out anew for today. In doing so, they have drawn closer to entering the minds of early Christians, with their lively appreciation of symbol and reality. In attempting to return to the roots of Christian symbolism, theologians are thus restoring to us some of the humanity, vision and beauty that has been lost over the centuries.

Natural Symbols

The symbol world of the early Christians and of the medieval Church grew out of that of ancient cultures. Ancient Jewish and other Near Eastern religions were rich in symbols, for these peoples were highly aware of the natural world which surrounded them. Bread and water, wine and oil, sun and moon, fire and light, rock, tree and serpent were important phenomena in their lives. They reappear in their myths and rituals in many forms. Ancient Near Eastern scriptures tell the story of the world's creation and of its destruction by water. In ancient Jewish rituals birds and animals were offered to God, and bread and wine were shared in communion. Jewish scriptures use a wealth of natural symbols to describe their experience of God. He falls on them like gentle, fertilising rain:

> He shall descend like rain on the meadow,
> like raindrops on the earth (*Psalm 71*.v.6).

God shines on his people with healing light:

> For you the sun of justice will shine out
> with healing in its rays (*Malachi* 4.2).

Early Christians retained these natural symbols. In their underground catacomb paintings are doves and peacocks, sheep and lambs with their shepherds, vines and wine-pressers and fishermen with their nets and rods. Christ was their fruitful vine and their good shepherd. As followers of Christ they saw themselves as doves and shepherded lambs, as fish caught in the net of the Church. Water themes abound: Noah in his ark saved by God from the disastrous flood, Moses striking the barren rock to bring forth life-giving water, and Jonah spewed out of the sea on to the land of eternal life.

Symbols help us to apprehend reality, and so they feature in most religions of the world, in their teaching and their worship. In different centuries, however, people respond with more or less sensitivity to symbols, and in the course of time symbols used in ritual may speak with diminished clarity. As worshippers lose a sense of the power inherent in natural symbols, they concentrate on spiritual meanings, and lose touch with the strength of the symbol itself. Take bread, for example. Jesus chose a powerful symbol from his people's experience, bread, their staple food or, as his people called it, 'the staff of life'. Jesus broke bread and shared it with his friends saying 'Take this and eat it', to show how he was breaking open his own life to nourish them. Christians today repeat this action using tiny white wafers which in no way nourish them bodily. On this level, the power of the symbol is greatly diminished. In the same way, baptism originally meant immersion in the flowing or living water of a river or spring. The power of the flowing current mirrored the flow of life within the candidate's own body. The candidate was also anointed with oil from head to foot, as an athlete ready to run the race of life. Today's candidate for baptism experiences a trickle of water and a dab of oil. Prayers said over the candidate explain the meaning of each gesture, but the symbols barely convey their message.

The Roots of Christian Symbols

This book is not a dictionary of sacramental theology, nor is it a psychological study of the meaning of symbols. Instead, it is an attempt to break through the layer of religious meanings that surround Christian symbols, in order to redis-cover the natural power of the symbols themselves. Their power is God-given and holy, for life itself is sacred. Many worshippers today mistrust the natural power of symbols, fearing it to be pagan, or not of God. Is a tree holy or not? Is bread holy or not? This book is written in the belief that every tree and all bread is holy because they are alive and life-giving. The power of symbols used in Christian worship is not conferred on them from outside by a magical interven-tion of God. Their power resides within them, for the Spirit of God is at home deep within every living thing. To the extent that we can prune away our accustomed layers of added meanings, we will rediscover Christian symbols in their naked power.

To do this we must explore the ancient roots of Christian symbols, without fear of their being pagan. In contrast to the 'cives' who lived in the town, the 'paganes' were those who lived in the countryside, in closer touch with the nourishing earth and the beauty of nature. Today the word 'pagan' has become a pejorative term which civilised people use when they are afraid to name ancient ways of seeing and doing things as human and therefore good. Accord-ing to the Oxford Dictionary, we commonly use the word 'pagan' when we mean 'unenlightened; irreligious'. It is easy to dismiss whole cultures as unen-lightened and irreligious, but we do so at the risk of cutting away our deepest roots. If we explore the ancient roots of Christian symbols without prejudice, we can come to a new appreciation of the reality contained within the great symbols of Christianity. We shall also strengthen bonds with our ancestors stretching back through thousands of years.

CHAPTER 2

Corn

The Bread of Life

The bread of life is perhaps the most intimate and most powerful Christian symbol. We eat bread and enter into communion with God through doing so, touching divinity through earthly matter. A tenth century desert father described what this felt like when he wrote:

> We hold in our hands not bread but fire.
> We gaze and eat, and see your invisible glory.

> (Simeon the New Theologian, transl. Maloney 1975, *Hymn 58*).

Sharing Divine Life

When Jesus stood in the synagogue at Capernaum and declared 'I am the bread of life' (John 6:35), we imagine him speaking out of the blue, inventing concepts to describe himself. Certainly, his listeners were confused by his statements, for in them Jesus was claiming godlike qualities, but the idea of sharing divine life through eating bread and drinking wine was ancient and widespread. Clement of Alexandria, for example, records a prayer from the worship of Cybele, the earth mother, in which the worshipper prayed:

> I have eaten from the timbrel,
> I have drunk from the cymbal,

describing a communion meal in which a wheaten cake symbolised the body of the divine son of Cybele, and blood or wine represented his life-blood (Harding 1971, pp136–137), for he was understood to be the fruit of the corn and the fruit of the vine. Jesus took to himself and deepened these concepts when he explained:

> My flesh is real food
> and my blood is real drink.
> He who eats my flesh and drinks my blood
> lives in me, and I live in him (*John* 6:55,56).

The ancient Israelites experienced holy communion with God through eating bread and drinking wine. A priestly code book describes various foods made from corn to offer God in thanks, using recipes not far removed from our own for bread, scones, pancakes and roast corn: 'When you are going to offer an oblation of dough baked in the oven, the wheaten flour is to be prepared either in the form of unleavened cakes mixed with oil, or in the form of unleavened wafers spread with oil. If your offering is an oblation cooked on the griddle, the wheaten flour mixed with oil is to contain no leavening... If your offering is an oblation cooked in the pan, the wheaten flour is to be prepared in oil... If you offer the Lord an oblation of first fruits, you must offer roasted corn or bread made from ground corn...' (*Leviticus* 2:4–15).

The ancient Israelites celebrated their springtime Passover by, among other things, eating unleavened bread for a week (*Exodus* 12:15–20), and pagan Greeks and Romans ate small cakes of wheat flour marked with a cross as a symbol of life, particularly at the festival of Diana at the spring equinox. Two petrified loaves with a cross on them were discovered in the ruins of Herculaneum, baked in 79 AD for some ritual purpose. The early Saxons seem to have eaten similar cakes at the same time in March, and they have become our hot cross buns. For centuries, English housewives rose at dawn on Good Friday to bake their round, spiced cakes with a cross, and bakers in the last century baked them through the night so that street vendors in London and other towns could sell them early on Good Friday morning (Hole 1976, p.185). Pre-Christian springtime cakes survive in various forms across Europe. On Shrove Tuesday, the day before the Lenten fast begins, doughnuts are baked in Vienna, as they were in Baldock, Hertfordshire. Small shell-shaped currant loaves were baked in Norwich. In Scotland, oatmeal bannocks were baked on a griddle before the whole family, servants, friends and neighbours. In England, pancakes were made, enabling the housewife to empty her larder of butter and fats before the Lenten fast. On the fourth Sunday of Lent, simnel cakes were eaten, baked to different recipes in different towns. The name 'simnel' comes from the Latin 'simila', describing the fine wheaten flour from which they are made (Hole 1976, pp.270, 279).

The Start of Corn-growing

Wheat and barley grew wild in the near and middle east around 8000 BC, when early farmers discovered that these grasses could provide fodder for their animals and food for themselves, once the ripe grasses had been bruised and soaked. The women in these small early farming communities used a primitive method of agriculture: they roughly prepared the ground with a notched stick to help the grasses grow. When the soil had been exhausted, these farmers moved on to another site. Some migrated westwards, and others settled in the fertile Nile valley, where emmer wheat seeds have been found preserved in grain storage pits. A settlement has recently been discovered off the coast at Haifa dating from 6000 BC, when farming was just beginning in Palestine, in which lentils and emmer wheat were grown, cut with sickles and ground with pestles and mortars (Galili, Kaufman and Weinstein-Evron 1988, pp.66–67).

In about 4000 BC, nomadic farmers migrated to Scandinavia and southern England. A Teutonic legend suggests that wheat was brought by sea from another country: the harvest goddess Freya, after whom Friday is named, gave a sheaf of golden corn to Heimdal, the keeper of the rainbow bridge, as a baby. He floated to Scedeland with his head pillowed on the wheat sheaf. When he reached the shore, people found him and brought him up, and he taught them how to grow seed from the sheaf. At the end of his human life, he asked them to put his body in a similar boat and set it afloat. They did this, putting thank offerings for the harvest all around him, and left the boat to drift away (Lambeth 1974, p.3). The legend ends by describing a ship burial like that of Sutton Hoo, in which a leader is buried together with offerings for his journey to the afterlife.

Water Germinates the Seed

In dry countries, water was essential to make the corn grow, and in Egypt and Babylon the harvest was considered to be a gift from the river. A fish deity, Rem, whose name means 'to weep', was thought to weep fertilising tears, and an Egyptian rain god, Tefnut, was called 'the spitter'. Gods spit seeds in American Indian kiva paintings. Early corn deities were often represented weeping, and because people realised the necessity of moisture to germinate the seeds, it was considered part of some sowing rituals that the sower should weep (Lambeth 1974, p.2). Psalm 126 takes up this theme, and applies it to the Jews going sadly into exile and then joyfully returning:

> Those who went sowing in tears
> now sing as they reap.
> They went away, went away weeping,
> carrying the seed.
> They come back, they come back singing,
> carrying their sheaves (*Psalm* 126:5,6).

In Babylon, Ishtar, the mother of the universe, supplied food for people and animals, and her son Tammuz became the corn spirit. He was a young god who died each year and returned to life, as the spirit of the seed which awoke to life and growth after the spring sowing. Similarly in Scandinavia, Thor fought and overcame the frost giants. Zeus, like the corn spirits of other lands, was said to die a violent death each year and be reborn in the cycle of ploughing, sowing and reaping. Each of these corn spirits received offerings: first human sacrifice, later that of animals and then, with the growth of civilisation, food and drink made from the newly harvested grain. Most peoples offered the first fruits of the harvest to their god, and it was usual to decorate the offering (Lambeth 1974, p.2). In the ancient story of Cain and Abel, the two brothers offer the first fruits of their grain and flocks to God (*Genesis* 4:1–4). Later, the Israelites codified this custom; in the Book of *Leviticus*, God tells his people: 'When you enter the land that I give you, and gather in the harvest there, you must bring the first sheaf of your harvest to the priest, and he is to present it to the Lord with the gesture of offering... You are to eat no bread, roasted corn or baked bread before this day, before making the offering to your God' (*Leviticus* 23:10–14). In medieval England, before the harvest proper, bread made from the first new corn of the year was brought to church and offered at Mass as a thanksgiving for the first fruits of the harvest. This happened on Lammas Day, which was 1st August or the Sunday nearest it. The word may derive from the Anglo-Saxon 'hlafmaesse' or 'loaf Mass' (Hole 1976, p.178).

Corn's Cycle of Growth

Corn was seen by the early Israelites as one of God's great blessings. In an ancient formula, the patriarch Isaac blesses his son Jacob with

> dew from heaven, and the richness of earth,
> abundance of grain and wine (*Genesis* 27:28).

In his turn, Jacob blesses his son Joseph with

> Blessings of breasts and womb,
> blessings of grain and flowers (*Genesis* 49:25).

A later writer prays:

> May our barns overflow
> with every possible crop (*Psalm* 144:13).

One of the psalms describes the cycle of the corn's growth from the time when the rain makes the seeds grow until the harvest, which is brought in with singing and joyful shouting:

> You visit the earth and water it,
> you load it with riches;
> God's rivers brim with water
> to provide its grain.
> This is how you provide it:
> by drenching its furrows, by levelling its ridges,
> by softening it with showers, by blessing the first fruits.
> You crown the year with your bounty,
> abundance flows wherever you pass;
> the desert pastures overflow,
> what shouts of joy, what singing! (*Psalm* 65:9–13).

The World Harvest

The Jewish people came to see the harvest as a symbol of God harvesting us. We grow like corn, and when we are ripe, God sends his messengers, his angels, to harvest us. The quality of the crop of the world may be good or bad; the prophet Joel thinks the crop harvested from Israel's enemies will be a bad one. He depicts God sending down his champion warriors and ordering them:

> Put the sickle in:
> the harvest is ripe;
> come and tread:
> the winepress is full,
> the vats are overflowing,
> so great is their wickedness! (*Joel* 4:13).

Corn and wine have here become human flesh and blood. The people of Israel will help God in this work of harvesting. Isaiah tells the weakened, exiled Israelites:

> Do not be afraid...
> See, I turn you into a threshing sled,
> new, with doubled teeth;
> you shall thresh and crush the mountains,
> and turn the hills to chaff.
> You shall winnow them and the wind will blow them away,
> the gale will scatter them (*Isaiah* 41:14–16).

In the Book of *Revelation*, John takes up the same theme of the harvest of God's enemies. An angel orders a heavenly reaper to set to work: 'Then another angel came out of the sanctuary, and shouted aloud to the one sitting on the cloud: "Put your sickle in and reap: harvest time has come and the harvest of the earth is ripe." Then the one sitting on the cloud set his sickle to work on earth, and the earth's harvest was reaped' (*Revelation* 14:15,16). Jesus, however, does not pursue this triumphalist theme, but sees the world's harvest in a more positive light. He also demystifies this strand of thinking by explaining that he and his followers are really doing the harvesting. He says to them: 'The harvest is rich but the labourers are few, so ask the Lord of the harvest to send labourers to his harvest' (*Matthew* 9:38). In a moment of excitement, when he has just converted the woman at the well, Jesus breaks out happily:

> Have you not got a saying:
> Four months and then the harvest?
> Well, I tell you:
> Look around you, look at the fields;
> already they are white, ready for harvest!
> Already the reaper is being paid his wages,
> already he is bringing in the grain for eternal life,
> and thus sower and reaper rejoice together (*John* 4:35–36).

Jesus often talked about growing corn: he saw it as a symbol of us growing. In the parable of the sower he describes the farmer broadcasting his seed (as happens still in some parts of Britain). Some falls on rich soil and grows well, but some falls on the path or among thorns and cannot grow (*Mark* 4:3–9). As the corn grows, weeds grow too. In another parable, the master's servants ask if they should pull out the weeds, but Jesus knows enough about farming to make the master say: 'No, because when you weed out the darnel, you might pull up the wheat with it. Let them both grow till the harvest; and at harvest time I shall say to the reapers: First collect the darnel and tie it into bundles to be burned, then gather the wheat into my barn' (*Matthew* 13:24–30). Reapers in England separated out the darnel, or vetch, by hand until combine harvesters began to be used. In Herefordshire in the last century, parties went out into the fields at Easter to pick corn cockles out of the fields. In some places groups were sent to pick the wild oats out of the cornfields, a process known in Oxfordshire as 'rogueing'.

Jesus was sensitive to the different phases of corn's growth from seed to ear, and he explained that we grow in the same natural way. 'He said: " This is what the kingdom of God is like. A man throws seed on the land. Night and day, while he sleeps, when he is awake, the seed is sprouting and growing; how, he does not know. Of its own accord the land produces first the shoot, then the ear, then the full grain in the ear. And when the crop is ready, he loses no time: he starts to reap because the harvest has come".' (*Mark* 4:26–29). In this parable, Jesus invites his hearers to start working for God, the Lord of the harvest.

Lord of the Harvest

The phrase 'Lord of the harvest' is not an abstract one. Until recently in Britain, the head worker's title was 'captain of the reapers' or 'Lord of the harvest'. He supervised the harvest, but his job was not merely practical; it was intimately bound up with the mystery of the life and death of the corn, which in turn gave food, and therefore life, to people. In parts of England until recently, at the end of the harvest the Lord of the harvest stood in the middle of the field, the workers doffed their hats and bowed down crying a mournful phrase three times, as the Lord of the harvest bent down and touched the ground with the last sheaf of corn. It was then raised high above the crowd, to a joyful cry. This appears to be the remains of an ancient ceremony enacting the death of fertility for the year and its rebirth next spring (Women's Institute 1979, p.12).

A similar ceremony was perhaps the basis of Joseph's dream in the Book of Genesis: 'Now Joseph had a dream, and he repeated it to his brothers. "Listen," he said, "to this dream I have had. We were binding sheaves in the countryside; and my sheaf, it seemed, rose up and stood upright; then I saw your sheaves gather round and bow to my sheaf." "So you want to be king over us," his brothers retorted, "or to lord it over us?"' (*Genesis* 37:5–8). Joseph dreamt he was Lord of the harvest, as he later became for the whole of Egypt when famine struck.

The Last Sheaf

The earliest form of this ritual was probably one involving human sacrifice, in which the reaper who cut the last sheaf, or a stranger representing him, would be killed on the field to restore life to the corn spirit who had died when the last sheaf was cut. As the field was reaped, the corn spirit was felt to retreat into the last bit of grain still standing, so the last sheaf became important, and risky to cut. In Britain it was often considered unlucky to cut it, and the cutter, though no longer sacrificed, would be swathed in the corn he had cut, jostled, bumped on the field and roughly handled. On some farms, to spread the responsibility for this dangerous act, the last sheaf was cut jointly: a little of the uncut corn was left standing and its stalks tied or plaited together. The reapers stood round it in a wide half circle, and one by one threw their sickles at it (Hole 1976, pp.135–136).

The ceremony of bowing to the sheaf then followed on many farms. It was called 'crying the neck', for the last sheaf of corn was called the neck. In 1826 a north Devon farmer wrote: 'I have once or twice heard upwards of twenty men cry it (the neck), and sometimes joined by an equal number of female voices. About three years back, on some high grounds, where our people were harvesting, I heard six or seven necks cried in one night, although I knew that some of them were four miles off. They are heard through the quiet evening air, at a considerable distance sometimes'. He adds, 'I think that the practice is beginning to decline of late, and many farmers and their men do not care about keeping up the old custom. I shall always practise it myself, because I take it in the light of a thanksgiving' (Hole 1976, pp.136–137). How did they 'cry the neck'? One observer wrote: 'As the captain of the reapers bent down and touched the ground with the last clump of corn, the assembled company would bow down crying "Wee Yew, Way Yew" three times. The clump (or 'neck') was then raised high above the crowd to shouts of "We have ye!", (Women's Institute 1979, p.12).

The Lord of the harvest or an old, respected worker would then fashion the last sheaf into a corn symbol or dolly, in order to preserve the life of the corn until next season. It might be made into a miniature sheaf, a spiral pyramid, or a design of plaits and hanging ears, or more often into the form of a female doll, tied with ribbons, with hair and hands made of ears of wheat (Hole 1976, p.137). These were made in Kent until recently, where they were called Ivy Maids. The doll was carried home with the last harvest load to the harvest supper in the farmhouse kitchen, and for the rest of the year she stayed there near the fireplace or in the barn, as a blessing on the farm. In the spring the doll was often returned to the land: she was broken up and mixed with the new seed to be sown, or sometimes fed to the first horses to go out and plough the fields (Women's Institute 1979, p.7). In some places she was kept not on the farm but in the parish church, where she still appears. At Little Waltham in Essex, she is fixed to a pew during the harvest festival. At Overbury in Worcestershire, a pyramid of twisted corn with wheat ears hanging from its base is hung in the church porch and renewed, not every year, but when necessary (Hole 1976, p.138). In Greek Orthodox countries, she generally remained in the church porch and was not allowed further into the church, but in Catholic countries, the Virgin Mary often took over attributes of the life- bringing corn maiden, and intricate straw work is still found around figures of Our Lady in rural areas of Catholic countries (Women's Institute 1979, p.48).

Corn Dollies: Symbols of Life

Corn dollies are extremely ancient, and the forms in which they are made have varied little for thousands of years. The oldest design is that of the spiral: this is a pre-Egyptian fertility symbol, which appears in many cultures. It can be found in Maltese temple decorations dated 3600 BC. The spiral may represent the whirlwind which heralds the rain. After the intense drought, just before the rains break, the air becomes sultry and dust eddies are whipped up, spiralling into the sky. Heavy rains follow, and the corn seeds can germinate. The word 'doll' comes from 'idol', and corn dollies were the earliest dolls, for small fertility images of corn were fashioned in ancient Mesopotamia. Corn dollies also became the first mobiles: they were hung over the dining table and in the larder in both ancient and modern Egyptian homes as a sign of blessing (Rees 1990).

Corn dollies were made in Egypt from the 18th dynasty (1570–1320 BC) in the shape of the Egyptian hieroglyph for life. This is a loop over a T, which the Egyptians called the Ankh, and the early Christians adopted as the Tau cross. Our crucifix, the Christian sign of life, comes from this symbol. In paintings in the pyramids, the god Osiris presents this symbol to pharaoh and his wife to indicate their new immortal state. Since hieroglyphs derive from natural symbols, and the corn dolly represents life, it is possible that the ankh corn dolly was the origin of the hieroglyph, since it follows the natural shape of corn stalks tied together. Corn dollies in the shape of the ankh, or tau cross, are still made in Morocco (Rees 1990).

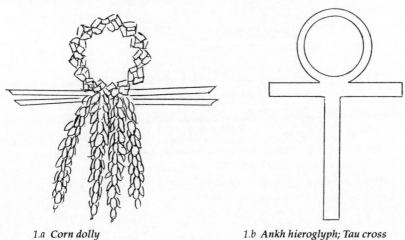

1.a *Corn dolly*   1.b *Ankh hieroglyph; Tau cross*

2. *'The bride of the corn': a design from Fez,*
Morocco. The bride represents the life of
of the corn. Photograph: Margaret Rees

3. **Straw crucifix from Mexico.**
Photograph: Margaret Rees

4. **Preparing decorated wedding loaves in the bakery, Anougia, Crete.** *A loaf in the form of a*
ring symbolises undying love. Photograph: Margaret Rees.

We assume that making the sign of the cross is a Christian tradition only, but in the 6th century BC the prophet Ezekiel pictures God telling his angels to mark the foreheads of people with the life-giving tau cross sign. He says: '"Go all through the city, all through Jerusalem, and mark a cross on the foreheads of all who deplore and disapprove of all the filth practised in it". I heard him say to others: "Follow him through the city and strike. Show neither pity nor mercy... But do not touch anyone with a cross on his forehead"' (*Ezekiel* 9:4–6). Around 95 AD, St. John takes up the same theme in *Revelation*. An angel orders the destroying angels at the end of time: 'Wait before you do any damage on land or at sea or to the trees, until we have put the seal on the foreheads of the servants of our God' (*Revelation* 7:3).

Cornucopia, the Horn of Plenty

Another ancient design for corn dollies is called the cage: within the ears of corn a hollow cage is constructed to provide a home for the corn spirit. This design was brought by the Arabs to Spain, where it is known today as the Spanish cage. In Sweden and other Scandinavian countries, its equivalent is known as 'the heart of the corn', which may be in the shape of a heart. Another ancient design is the cornucopia: a horn of plenty, filled with the different heads of grain grown on the farm (wheat, barley, oats, rye) and other nuts, seeds, fruit and flowers, all encased in a horn-shaped casket of woven straw. In ancient Greece, the cornucopia was supposed to be the creation of Zeus. He wanted a thank offering for the nymphs who had cared for him as a baby, so he took a ram's horn and filled it with the finest edible seeds, giving it to them with the promise that it would provide all the food they needed. The origin of the horn of plenty, however, was probably the ancient belief that the fertility of animals resided in their horns, whose crescent shape linked them with the moon goddess.

In a cornucopia corn dolly found in Guatemala, seven full ears of corn represent a full harvest, since seven is an ancient number of completion. The theme of seven full ears of corn representing a full harvest is the subject of another dream in the story of Joseph in the Book of *Genesis*. Pharaoh dreams: '"In my dream, there, growing on one stalk, were seven ears of corn, beautifully ripe; but sprouting up after them came seven ears of corn, withered, meagre and scorched by the east wind. The shrivelled ears of corn swallowed the seven ripe ears of corn"...' Joseph explains to pharaoh: '"The seven ripe ears of corn are seven years... Seven years are coming, bringing great plenty to the whole land of Egypt, but seven years of famine will follow them...when famine will exhaust the land"' (*Genesis* 41:22–30). Pharaoh then asks Joseph to take command during the seven wonderful harvests, and Joseph stores enough grain to feed the country during the ensuing famine.

Harvest Celebrations

In most countries where cereals are grown, the last sheaf from the harvest is preserved in some form. In Burma, rice plant stalks are fashioned into a rice mother. In southern France, palm leaves are shredded and fashioned into a doll. In Ireland, rushes are used to make countrymen's favours (to give their girl-friends as a token of fertility) and St. Bridget's crosses. St. Bridget's cross is the Irish dolly; legend says that as Bridget watched by the bedside of her dying father, she idly picked up some of the rushes covering the floor and wove them into a cross. Her father asked what she was doing, and when she explained the meaning of the cross to him, he was converted (Rendell 1976, p.47). In England, when the last sheaf in the last field was ready to be cut, and the corn dolly made from it, ribbons to decorate her were taken out to the field. Their colours had meanings: some varied according to the county, but in general, white ribbons represented the virgin spirit of the corn, in the same way that a white ribbon is tied round the horseshoe at a wedding to symbolise the bride's purity. The colour most commonly used was red, the colour of spilt blood, reminiscent of blood sacrifice in earliest harvest rituals. From ancient times, cornfields were streaked with scarlet poppies, and they in turn came to represent spilt blood. On Poppy Day they represent the blood of soldiers slain in the cornfields of France. In the same way, red vestments at Mass represent the spilt blood of martyrs.

5. *Harvest Home in England: the harvesters celebrate, while a woman carries the last sheaf.*
  (*Drawing by Steven Nemethy, based on an old engraving*)

Since the harvest was the result of most of the year's work, its completion was marked by a great celebration. The harvest supper was held in a barn; the corn dolly was hung up in a prominent place, and seats of honour reserved for the man who had woven it and the woman who had carried it home. Trials of strength, dancing and drinking went on. In some places the Lord of the harvest collected money to provide for extra drink at harvest time. The harvest festival began only in 1843 when the vicar of Morwenstow, Cornwall decided to revive the ancient Lammas thanksgiving service, now no longer in thanks for the first corn but for the end of the harvest. Since harvest suppers were rowdy occasions, they began to be replaced by this church service followed by a large supper for all the parishioners, paid for by the farmers and tradesmen. The bread, fruit and vegetables from the harvest festival were taken afterwards to hospitals and local charities (Hole 1976, p.139).

Threshing and Winnowing

When the corn was gathered in, it had to be threshed and winnowed. Some Arab villages in Israel today still have a communal threshing floor which is a compound at the end of the village where each farmer threshes his pile of grain. There is an interesting description of activities around the threshing floor in the Old Testament book of *Ruth*. A Jewish law gave the poor the right to glean at harvest time, if the landowner allowed it, and Ruth, the great-grandmother of King David, met her future husband, Boaz, by gleaning in his barley fields at harvest time. Boaz invited her to sit with the reapers, and made a heap of roasted grain for her, telling her: 'Come, eat some of this bread and dip your piece in the wine'. Since Boaz knew who she was, he ordered his servants: 'Let her glean among the sheaves themselves, and do not check her. And see you pull a few ears of corn from the bundles and let them fall. Let her glean them, and do not scold her' (*Ruth* 2:14–17).

That night, Boaz winnowed the barley at the threshing floor, along with the other winnowers. The story continues: 'When Boaz had eaten and drunk, he was in a happy mood and went to lie down by the heap of barley. Then Ruth came quietly and turned back the covering at his feet and lay there. In the middle of the night the man started up and looked about him; and there lying at his feet was a woman'. In this way Ruth offered to become his wife and raise an heir to continue the family line, but Boaz prudently sent her away at daylight: 'She lay at his feet till morning. Boaz rose before the hour when one man can recognise another, "For," said he, "it must not be known that this woman came to the threshing floor". Then he said to her, "Bring the cloak you are wearing and hold it out". She held it out while he put six measures of barley into it and then gave it to her to carry' (*Ruth* 3:1-15). This story conveys the happiness, plenty and fertility that harvest brings.

6. *Harvest dance, Sicily, in which the community asks for a fruitful harvest. 1. Women kneel beside their sheaves. They mime sowing seed, while men mime cutting corn.* Photograph: Margaret Rees.

7. *Harvest dance, Sicily. 2. Haymaking: women carry pitchforks and men carry sickles.* Photograph: Margaret Rees.

8. *Harvest dance, Sicily. 3. Men winnow grain and brandish flails; women carry corn sheaves.* Photograph: Margaret Rees.

9. *Ancient Egyptian workers winnowing grain* (after a tomb painting in Thebes)

In times of war, harvesting was more difficult. Gideon threshed wheat inside the family winepress, to keep it hidden from the attacking Midianites (*Judges* 6:11). A fan was used for winnowing, or blowing, the chaff from the grain when threshing corn, and enemies were seen as chaff to be winnowed. John the Baptist described how Jesus would sift out the people with his winnowing fan: 'His winnowing fan is in his hand; he will clear his threshing floor and gather his wheat into the barn; but the chaff he will burn in a fire that will never go out' (*Matthew* 3:12). The ancient Greeks thought of Demeter, the corn goddess, as presiding over the threshing floor. Theocritus wrote of her: 'Ah, once again may I plant the great fan on her corn heap, while she stands smiling by, Demeter of the threshing floor, with sheaves and poppies in her hand' (Rendell 1976, p.48). In Morocco, corn dollies are still made in the shape of a winnowing fan.

Jesus as Bread of Life

Jesus inherited a rich variety of traditions centred around corn, the bread of life, and since he lived close to a number of trade routes and surrounded by several cultures, he would have been aware of these traditions. He often taught using corn, as we have seen. He encouraged his hungry friends to eat ears of corn in defiance of Jewish sabbath rules, and he blessed and multiplied bread for the crowds who followed him, feeding them not only with life-giving words but also with life-giving bread. In his most complex homily in the tiny synagogue at Capernaum, Jesus explained that he was the true bread of life, the bread of heaven who feeds the world with life. At his Last Supper he urged his friends to break bread and eat it as a communion or sharing in his life which he had already fully spent on them.

But Jesus insisted on the full reality of the symbol of bread made from corn. He knew that death is necessary for deeper life, and he explained this mystery of growth: 'Unless a wheat grain falls on the ground and dies, it remains only a single grain, but if it dies, it yields a rich harvest' (*John* 4:35–36). Jesus was the inheritor and culmination of the ancient and worldwide belief in a divine figure killed and reborn in the spring, as the grain is harvested and sown again. Jesus would not have allowed the harvester of the last sheaf in the field to be sacrificed to bring new life for the following year, but there is a deep element of truth in this action, and Jesus allowed himself to be sacrificed to bring new life. In Mexico a beautiful straw crucifix is made, in which Christ's body is fashioned from woven straw, and he is adorned with a straw halo and crown of thorns. In this dolly, life and death are bound together in a simple but awesome proclamation that life moves through death into fuller life, through the creative power of God.

A modern English Easter hymn describes the wheat that is Christ rising to life anew each springtime:

> Now the green blade riseth
> from the buried grain,
> wheat that in the dark earth
> many days has lain;
> love lives again,
> that with the dead has been:
> love is come again
> like wheat that springeth green.
>
> In the grave they laid him,
> Love whom men had slain,
> thinking that never
> he would wake again,
> laid in the earth
> like grain that sleeps unseen:
> Love is come again
> like wheat that springeth green.

Forth he came at Easter,
like the risen grain,
he that for three days
in the grave had lain,
quick from the dead
my risen Lord is seen:
love is come again
like wheat that springeth green.

(Crum 1977, *Hymn S3*)

CHAPTER 3

Water and Blood
The Ark of Safety

There is an ancient American Indian prayer chant which begins:

> O mother earth and father sky,
> Your children are we, and with tired backs
> We bring you the gifts you love.
> Then weave for us a garment of brightness,
> O mother earth and father sky (Astrov 1962 p.221).

We are familiar with the concept of mother earth, but less familiar with that of father sky. American Indians spoke of father sky because they could see how mother earth's children grew with the sun's light and the rain's moisture. An American Indian creation myth describes how sky met earth in a storm, and the world was filled with the children to whom they gave birth.

Rain Unites Earth and Heaven

The fertilising storm or cloudburst was the subject of other myths. Jan Gossaert was a 16th century Flemish artist who normally painted reverent madonnas and saints. In an unusual picture he illustrates the ancient Greek myth of Danae, a young woman who was impregnated by Zeus in the form of a golden shower. The myth reflects the symbolism of the cloudburst as a sacred marriage between heaven and earth (Jacobi 1964, p.280). In Gossaert's painting, Danae sits receptively in her house as the golden shower descends on her. A church visible through Danae's window emphasises the holiness of the scene. The picture echoes annunciation paintings of the time, in which the angel Gabriel tells Mary that God's Spirit will overshadow her, and so she will conceive. Other myths describe rain as a union of love between heaven and earth. In the Greek Eleusinian mysteries, after everything had been purified with water, the call went up to heaven: 'Let it rain!' and down to earth: 'Be fruitful!' This was understood as a sacred marriage of the gods (Jacobi 1964, p.281).

Canaanite people shared this awe for earth and sky, and the Israelites who lived among them developed similar concepts. God tells the heavens to rain; they do so, and earth responds with fruitful growth. Hosea (6th century BC), a Jewish prophet influenced by Canaanite culture, preaches: 'In those days, says the Lord, I shall answer the heavens; they shall answer the earth; it shall answer grain, wine, oil' (*Hosea* 2.23–24). A psalm expresses this more formally:

> The Lord will make us prosper
> and our earth shall yield its fruit.
> Faithfulness shall spring from the earth
> and justice look down from heaven (*Psalm 84*, 12, 13).

The Flood Which Renews

Rain can be creative or destructive. The story of the flood is one of many myths of cosmic disaster which explain the decay and renewal of the earth. Widely separated peoples told stories of a great flood which, long ago, overwhelmed vast stretches of land and great cities, and drowned everyone except one man with his family. In the oldest forms of this legend, the whole world is inundated. The man builds or finds a ship and, after a time, when the gods have stopped being angry, the waters recede, and the hero fills the world with his descendants and with the animals that sailed with him. A great Old Testament story is that of Noah's ark (*Genesis* 6–9). Because the world had grown evil, God sent a huge flood to destroy everything, and made a new start with his servant Noah. This story comes from a much older Mesopotamian legend which Abraham's people perhaps brought with them when they migrated to Canaan. The oldest known version of the story is inscribed on a stone tablet dated around 2100 BC from Nippur in Sumeria (*Encyclopaedia of World Mythology* 1970, p.37). Flood legends may date back to the end of the pleistocene era, when vast ice sheets melted, causing a rise in sea level and flooding such low-lying areas as Mesopotamia.

Early stories of the flood are related to the moon, who mysteriously causes the tides and flooding. The Babylonian moon goddess Ishtar both caused the great flood and saved the remnant of her people. In 'The eleventh tablet of creation' she laments over her threatened children, and then saves them in a boat which she makes like Noah's ark. When the storm recedes, she sends out a dove and, later, all the animals:

> Six days and nights passed.
> The wind, the deluge, storm overwhelmed.
> On the seventh day in its course
> was calmed the storm and all the deluge
> which had destroyed like an earthquake,
> quieted...
> On the seventh day, in the course of it,
> I sent forth a dove and it left...
> I sent the animals forth to the four winds (Smith 1873–81, p.159).

The dove, a bird often associated with the moon goddess, also leads Noah out onto dry land. Noah is probably a form of Nuah, an even earlier Babylonian moon goddess who also built an ark, a crescent-shaped boat, in which she could carry a few of her children, the seed of all living things, over the flood which she had caused.

The Moon Boat: An Ark of Safety

Below are two illustrations of moon boats, the first ancient Egyptian and the second from Ur of the Chaldees, which was the home of Abraham, the father of the Jewish nation. The Egyptian boat contains the moon, and is guarded by the two eyes of Horus, symbolising the moon's light. The eyes of God are still painted on the prows of Maltese fishing boats as a blessing. In the boat from Ur (dated 2300–2100 BC), the moon god is paddling across the sky. There are similar Assyrian pictures showing the moon god Sinn paddling his crescent boat across the sky. Sinn gave his name to Mount Sinai (or moon mountain), the sacred mountain which Moses climbed to receive God's message (Harding 1971, pp.90, 222).

The word 'ark' means the arc of a circle; it also means 'crescent', as in crescent moon, for Noah's ark is a moon boat, carrying souls to a new world and a new incarnation; it is the boat of immortality. In Christianity it became the boat of

10. *Ancient Egyptian moon boat. (Drawing by Stephen Nemethy)*

11. *Moon boat, or ark, from Ur of the Chaldees. (Drawing by Stephen Nemethy)*

the Church, carrying its people safely to heaven. A ship is one of the earliest symbols of the Church sailing unharmed through all perils. The anchor was an early Christian symbol of the stability of the Church: it is found in wall paintings in the catacombs. The word 'nave' (the part of the church building in which the people gather) comes from the Latin 'navis' or ship.

In Greek mythology, the boat which ferries souls to the other world is guided by Charon the boatman. He ferries the souls of the dead across the river Styx to Hades. Sometimes in later European paintings he ferries the Holy Family to safety as they flee into Egypt. A parallel figure is St. Christopher, who possibly lived in Asia Minor in the third century. His name means 'Christ bearer'. He was a giant who lived beside a river and carried travellers across it on his shoulders including, on one occasion, the child Christ. He was invoked for protection against water and tempests, and remains a popular patron of travellers. Many English wall paintings of St. Christopher survive in medieval churches. They are usually on the north wall opposite the church porch, where grateful travellers could see Christopher at a glance.

The rescue of drowning people is another aspect of the ark story. St. Nicholas, a fourth century bishop in Asia Minor, took on this aspect of the story. He is the patron of sailors because, in one legend, he is invoked (after his death) by sailors whose boat is sinking. Nicholas appears overhead and calms the storm. Nicholas was the most popular bishop in the medieval Church; almost four hundred English churches are dedicated to him, most of them around the coast (Vince 1969, p.24). Christopher and Nicholas thus became the heroes who took on Noah's role in medieval Christianity.

The Moon Goddess is Christianised
What happened to the moon goddess in Christianity? She became St. Ursula. Ursula was a fourth century virgin who was probably martyred with her companions by barbarians in Cologne, Germany. Her eleven companions were mistranslated, and became a company of 11,000 virgins. Ursula's popularity grew enormously as she took over and christianised the properties of the virgin goddess, especially after the eleventh century. In the later Middles Ages a custom grew of founding guilds in Germany, especially along the Rhine and in Swabia, called 'Skiffs of St. Ursula'. These skiffs were for men and women, directed by monks, normally Carthusians, who served as captain, mate and pilot of each boat. To join the skiff, one had to say certain prayers, to help stock the boat's hold. For example, a Strasbourg skiff in 1480 was loaded with 180,000 prayers on the Passion of Christ, 76,000 bodily penances, 35,000 vigil services for the dead, 11,000 Our Fathers and 6530 Hail Marys in honour of St. Ursula, and so on. The passengers could draw on these provisions, and popes granted special indulgences to those who sailed in St. Ursula's skiffs. The boats were drawn in procession through the streets and, as recently as a hundred years ago,

boats could still be seen, decorated with flags, pulled through the streets of Rhineland towns at carnival time. In Brussels and Boulogne, the ship contained a statue of Our Lady (Baring-Gould 1897, p.353).

This custom existed long before St. Ursula's legend. Tacitus describes a ship carried around in honour of the goddess Isis on 5th March when winter storms at sea are over, in thanks that the ocean can be sailed again. The ship was laden with the first fruits of spring. The German Church condemned the carrying round of this ship, except when it was connected with St. Ursula, who was considered to have christianised the custom. The Germans called the goddess Isis Hörsel, who sailed out of Engeland (the land of Engels) in Scandinavia. From this arose the legend that Ursula came from England. The names most frequently given to her companions were Vinnosa, Martha and Saula. Ursula's leading virgin seems to have been Vinnosa because in Scandinavia, Isis became Vana, or goddess of the Vans. Martha and Saula were probably 'Mârten und Seelen', spirits and souls who accompanied the goddess Hörsel everywhere. Hörsel was in fact the moon goddess, gliding in her silver skiff of a crescent moon over the blue sea of the sky, accompanied by her train of stars. In medieval Christianity, these became St. Ursula and her 11,000 virgins sailing across the sea of this life into eternity (Baring-Gould 1897, p.353).

From the ninth century onwards, churches throughout Europe were dedicated to Ursula and her company of virgins. Ursula became patroness of youth, since 'virgin' meant 'unmarried' at this time; and she was also patroness of universities throughout Europe: those places where the young studied. Considering her slight historical basis, her popularity in medieval Europe was remarkable. She seems to have answered a deep psychic need: our need to have, or indeed be, a virgin moon goddess, sailing across the sea of time into eternity.

Springs of Life

Water comes both from the heavens and from the earth. Since it is so necessary to life, springs, fountains and wells have always been revered. A spring makes the earth around it fertile, and provides water for people and animals to drink, and many cultures understand a spring to be the dwelling place of a good spirit. Springs were considered healing waters because they were the only pure drinking and cleansing places before modern sanitation and hygiene.

Wells in Britain were honoured with religious ceremonies and dances, and decorated with flowers and green branches at festivals. These ceremonies continued in Christian times, although most of the ancient wells were re-dedicated to Our Lady or one of the saints. Well-dressing has taken place intermittently in Derbyshire, at St. Anne's well in Buxton, for example. This is a Roman well which was known for its healing properties in medieval times. In 1538 one of Thomas Cromwell's agents destroyed it, together with 'crutches, shirts and shifts, with wax (candles) offered'. Within 40 years, Buxton became a spa noted for its medical cures. Today, three wells in Buxton are dressed with flowers and blessed on the Thursday nearest midsummer day (Christian 1987, p.9).

The New Year was experienced as a time of new beginnings and new life. In parts of Britain, the first water drawn from a well, pond or stream on New Year's morning was called the 'flower of the well' or the 'cream of the well'. Scottish farmers gave it to their cows to drink and washed their dairy utensils in it. Householders bottled it and kept it through the year as a blessing. People waited up to see the New Year in, and then ran to the well to be the first to draw water. In Northumberland, the first person to arrive would fill his pail and then throw some grass, hay or flowers into the well as an offering to the spring and a sign that the well was now creamed (Hole 1976, p.219).

At Sunday Mass, the priest blessed his people by sprinkling them with holy water. In South Wales, until the beginning of this century, boys went round the parish early on New Year's morning and carried out a similar ceremony. They brought fresh spring water with them and an evergreen twig, with which they sprinkled the face and hands of everyone they met. They went from house to house, sprinkling rooms and doors with their new water. As they did so, they chanted the following song, which retains its beauty although some of its words are corrupt:

> Here we bring new water from the well so clear,
> For to worship God with, this happy New Year.
> Sing levy dew, sing levy dew, the water and the wine,
> With seven bright gold wires, the bugles that do shine;
> Sing reign of fair maid, with gold upon her toe,
> Open you the west door, and turn the old year go;
> Sing reign of fair maid, with gold upon her chin,
> Open you the east door, and let the New Year in (Hole 1976, p.220).

Healing Waters

Roman writers tell us that the druids had sacred springs, pools and lakes, and made votive offerings of human heads to wells. After the druids were massacred by the Romans in Anglesey in 60 AD, Celtic Christians re-dedicated their wells to local saints. In Cornwall there are over 200 holy wells which, unlike those in other parts of Britain, are enclosed springs in which the water flows into a shallow basin. Over 40 of them are reputed to have healing qualities: various wells were efficacious for those with eye, skin or bowel diseases, for the lame, the mentally ill or for sick children. The patient was brought to the appropriate well in early May, the time of the pagan Celtic festival of growth and rebirth, Beltane. The patient would drink the water and sleep beside the well. Before departing, he would leave some strips of clothing in offering, tied to the branches of a nearby tree. As the cloth disintegrated, it was hoped that the illness would heal. The lame who were cured would leave their crutches beside the well in thanks. Today rags are still found tied to trees near Cornish wells (Leggat

1987, pp.1–6). These holy wells are a testimony to the belief of Cornish people over at least 2000 years that water brings life and health.

The Hebrew word for spring water is 'living water', water which brings life. A creation story in the book of Genesis describes a spring rising in the garden of Eden which becomes four mighty rivers, including the Tigris and the Euphrates (*Genesis* 2:10). These were the rivers which brought life to the fertile crescent. In the sixth century BC the prophet Ezekiel envisions a future time when a beautiful temple will again be built in Jerusalem. A stream will emerge from its foundations, flowing eastward from the right side of the temple. It will become a mighty river teeming with fish, bringing life and healing as it flows (*Ezekiel* 47:1–12). During the Jewish feast of Tabernacles, when life-giving water was a theme of the scripture readings and Ezekiel's prophecy was read, Jesus took up this theme. He stood in the temple precincts and cried out:

> If anyone is thirsty, let him come to me!
> Let the man come and drink who believes in me!
> As scripture says:
> 'From his breast shall flow fountains of living water' (*John* 7:38).

St. John reflected further about the river of life: he explained it as the stream of blood and water flowing out from the right side of the temple of the body of the crucified Christ (*John* 19:35–36). The early Church fathers developed this image: Christ on the cross was like a mother giving birth, and the Church was born in the stream of blood and water flowing from Christ as he slept in death.

Baptism

If the Church was born from this living water, how could a person join it? There had to be a way of immersing oneself in this water of death and emerging newborn. The word baptism means immersion. Baptising, or immersing, was a practice used by a number of ancient Jewish revivalists: you would go out to the river Jordan, where the preacher would immerse you as a sign of repentance and renewal. John the Baptist was doing this when his cousin Jesus came to him asking for baptism. The early Church fathers loved to think about this incident. What happened when the Son of God came asking for renewal? One explanation they gave was that Christ renewed the water, instead of the water renewing him. They said: Christ baptised by John in the Jordan blessed all the waters of the earth, since in time all waters touch one another. For water evaporates, falls as rain, flows through rivers into the sea and evaporates again in an endless cycle.

How were candidates baptised in the early Church? Some detailed accounts survive. St. Cyril, who was bishop of Jerusalem in the fourth century, has left us transcripts of his sermons to his candidates for baptism. These sermons may have been written nearer AD 600, under Cyril's name, but nonetheless provide an accurate account of early baptism. He instructed them daily during the 40 days of Lent, preaching in the Church of the Holy Sepulchre in Jerusalem. This was a dramatic place for him to explain about Christ dying for them and rising to bring them new life, since his church was built to enclose both the site of Calvary and the nearby site of the resurrection. Cyril explains that if the candidates persevere with their Lenten journey of faith, their Easter baptism will be a marvellous experience: 'On that night, heaven will be opened to each one of you. You will go down into those wonderful Christ-bearing waters; you will receive the name of Christian, and the capacity for understanding and appropriating the things of God... So when you see the water in the baptismal font, do not think of it as mere water; think of the saving power with which the Holy Spirit has endowed it' (Cyril 1977).

A third century pagan orator, Cyprian, described his baptism: 'At last I made up my mind to ask for baptism. I went down into those life-giving waters, and all the stains of my past were washed away. I committed my life to the Lord; he cleansed my heart, and filled me with his Holy Spirit. I was born again, a new man. Then, in a most marvellous way, all my doubts cleared up. I could now see what had been hidden from me before' (Cyprian 1977). Cyprian's conversion must have gone deep, for two years later he was elected bishop of Carthage.

Early texts describe the baptism ceremony, and two well-preserved ancient baptisteries in the Church of the Annunciation and the nearby Church of St. Joseph in Nazareth show us how Christians carried out baptism in the first four centuries. The candidate was led down into an underground grotto, 'like a snake slides into a hole' to change its skin, explained St. Cyril. He took off his clothes and sandals, as a sign that he renounced his former life and joined the struggle of Christ fighting naked on the cross against Satan. He stretched his hand towards the west, the direction of darkness, where the sun goes down, and declared: 'I renounce you, Satan, and all your following!' Then he turned to the east, the direction of sunrise and new light, and cried out to God: 'I believe and bow before you and all your servants, O Father, Son and Holy Spirit'. Oil lamps were then lit, and placed on rock shelves in the grotto. Many baptismal lamps were found near Bethlehem, bearing inscriptions such as 'The Lord is my light' and 'May the light of Christ the Lord appear!' (Briand 1982, pp.55–57).

The candidate was next anointed all over with oil and marked with the sign of the cross. He took an oil lamp and, guided by a deacon representing the archangel Michael, was led in procession through an underground passage to the baptistery with its sunken square basin and its mosaic floor. Female candidates were anointed and robed by a woman deacon. The baptistery in St. Joseph's church can be clearly seen, its seven steps still decorated with mosaics. The candidate descended the steps, as Christ went down into his tomb, acolytes representing the angels accompanying him. In Eastern Church art, when Christ is portrayed being baptised in the Jordan, angels surround him and watch over his clothes. The prominence of Michael and the other angels in this ancient ceremony may have inspired the role of godparents in present day baptism (Briand 1982, pp.57–62).

The River Jordan

Water flowed over the mosaic pavement, recalling the river Jordan which the candidate symbolically crossed to meet the bishop standing against the far wall. The bishop poured water over him three times, invoking the Father, Son and Holy Spirit. As the candidate climbed back up the steps, he recalled the miraculous descent of the Holy Spirit on Christ as he came up out of the Jordan: 'Immediately on coming up out of the water, he saw the sky rent in two and the Spirit resting on him like a dove' (*Mark* 1:10). The deacon then clothed him in a white robe as a symbol of renewal. He was crowned with a wreath of flowers, and fed with milk and honey just as, before Christianity, Roman children were given milk and honey as a sign that they had been received into the family (Jungmann 1960, p.139). The rite of baptism was thus a powerful experience, using many symbols to speak to the candidate on deep psychic levels.

Baptism was not seen as an isolated event. The new Christian should keep returning to the life-giving waters. As one Eastern father begs: 'Hurry to my Jordan!' Another, St. Theodore the Studite, preaches: 'Let us go in spirit to the Jordan, and there let us see the great light, our Christ, baptised. Let us kiss his fleeting traces in the water. Let us no more return to the shades of sin, but let us go forth and walk with him as true followers. And let us first receive baptism with him, I mean the baptism of tears, for it is in truth an ever shining purgation. From our depths come the waves. We too have a Jordan, illumined as we are by the flow of tears' (Hausherr 1982, p.131). The waters of the world include our tears. Tears are an expression of true emotion: we cry out in sorrow, and we cry for joy. The early Christian fathers prized what they called the gift of tears. In the sixth century, St. Benedict advised his monks when they went to chapel to 'go in simply and pray, but with tears and fervour of heart'. A friend of St. Dominic (13th century) described him at prayer with the same intense feeling. Sometimes 'he would weep and groan vehemently' while at other times he 'reflected an intense joy as he wiped away the flowing tears' (Tugwell 1978, pp.11,44).

In England we think of ourselves as reserved, but weeping has been part of our tradition. The medieval Sarum (Salisbury) Missal contains a Mass for tears, which begins with the following prayer: 'All powerful and merciful God, who brought forth a spring of living water from the earth for the thirsting people, draw forth tears of repentance from the hardness of our hearts...' (Atkinson 1983, pp.58–59). Margery Kempe was a fifteenth century Norfolk pilgrim and housewife who wept as she prayed. In her autobiography Margery writes of herself:

> She had these thoughts and these desires
> with profound tears, sighings and sobbings,
> and sometimes with great boisterous cries,
> as God would send it;

> and sometimes soft tears and secret,
> without any noise (Butler-Bowden 1936, p.82).

In this way Margery allowed the river of life to flow through her, and out into her world.

Blood, the Essence of life

If tears spring from our inner self, blood flows even deeper within us. In many cultures, blood equals life. Blood is the substance of life; its spilling brings death. Blood represents the place where life and death meet, and because it marks the frontier between life and death, it has often been a pathway of communication between people and God. In some cultures, human blood was spilt; societies with greater reverence for human life sacrificed animals instead. To sacrifice means to make something holy, or to do the holy thing. It is an attempt to bridge the chasm between our world and God, to reach into the unseen world where God lives, where human words cannot reach far enough. The sacrifice is transformed as it crosses the boundary between the two worlds. As the animal is slaughtered or the grain is burnt, it leaves the offerer irrevocably and passes over into the supernatural world. The offering must be whole and unblemished to cross over into the divine world as a representative of the offerer, so it was often the first fruits or the firstborn of the herd, representing all that the offerer hoped to receive (Schreiter 1988, pp.1–10).

Ancient Israel used animal sacrifice at important moments in her life. Moses bound his people to God in a blood ritual, as the book of Exodus describes. Young bulls were killed and their blood collected in large bowls. Half the blood was splashed on the altar and the other half sprinkled over the people. As Moses sprinkled them he proclaimed: 'This is the blood of the covenant which the Lord has made with you...' (*Exodus* 24:6–8). In this story, Moses flung half the bulls' blood against the altar to carry the message to God, and he sprinkled the other half on the people as a message from God that this band of slaves had now become God's special people. This blood made them a family and gave them a shared life and purpose.

Another blood ritual was enacted on the most solemn day of their year, the Day of Atonement. This was the day of their most intimate contact with God, as the high priest entered the heart of the sanctuary for the only time in the year, bearing sacrificial blood with which to renew the covenant between God and his people. Israelites believed that God was more powerfully present above the altar in the Holy of Holies than anywhere else in the world. Once a year the priest sprinkled blood on this altar as the most direct contact with the divine reality that Israel knew. On this day the people made a fresh start: their sins were lifted from them and ceremonially loaded upon a scapegoat, who was then driven out into the wilderness to die. The people felt forgiven, and able to draw close to God once more (*Leviticus* 16:1–34).

The Sacrificial Lamb

A young ram (hence 'lamb') was the normal sacrificial animal in family rituals. When a family offered a lamb, it was roasted, offered to God, and then eaten by the family with God's blessing, as a sign of life shared among the family, with God. Of these ritual meals, the most important for Israelite families was the passover meal, which took place each spring. This celebrated their passing over from slavery in Egypt to freedom under the leadership of Moses. They were able to escape after their God inflicted ten plagues on the Egyptians. In the last of these plagues, the firstborn in each Egyptian household died. The angel of death passed over the homes of the Israelites because each Jewish family had slaughtered a lamb and smeared its blood on their doorposts: its life-blood saved them (*Exodus* 12:1–14).

This blood ritual was in fact far older than the Exodus story. It was an ancient Egyptian springtime ritual, held at the beginning of the new year. In many cultures the transition from winter to spring was considered dangerous because the forces of death accumulated in the darkness of winter, and they might engulf the fragile forces of life coming to birth in the spring. At this time, special protection was necessary for people and animals against 'the destroyer', as Exodus puts it. Near Eastern peoples believed that animals' blood contained their God-given life-force, so the Egyptians protected themselves from the destroyer by anointing their doorways with blood. Blood on the doorpost of a house meant that the life within belonged to God, and the destroyer who wished to snatch it away would have to contend with God. The blood of a young innocent lamb emphasised the dramatic struggle between life and death. The Hebrews probably learnt this ritual in Egypt, and when they joined the other tribes at Shechem to form Israel (*Joshua* 24:1–18) it is likely that they brought this ritual with them in memory of how God had protected them (Schreiter 1988, p.3).

Jesus, the Lamb of God

Early Christians took over the symbol of the lamb with its blood. Using the language of the high priest on the Day of Atonement, John the Baptist says of Jesus: 'Look, there is the lamb of God that takes away the sin of the world!' (*John* 1:29). John the evangelist points out that Jesus died on the cross at the moment when the passover lambs were being slain in the temple (*John* 19:14), and quotes words from the passover preparation ritual as he describes the new passover lamb: 'Not one bone of his shall be broken' (*Exodus* 12:46; *John* 19:36). Finally, in his Book of Revelation, John pictures the heavenly worshippers adoring 'the lamb standing slain': the lamb sacrificed, yet standing in triumph (*Revelation* 5:6).

Christians developed this symbolism because their leader Jesus did so. At the end of his life, the gospels describe how he ate a final passover meal with his apostles. St. John, who was very sensitive to symbolism, noted: 'It was before the festival of passover, and Jesus knew that the hour had come for him to pass over from this world to the Father' (*John* 13:1). During the meal he took some bread, broke it and gave it to his friends to eat, inviting them to do the same in the future, remembering his broken body. He did the same with a cup of wine, the blood of the grape, using the language of the ancient covenant ritual to explain: 'This cup is the new covenant in my blood, which will be poured out for you' (*Luke* 22:20). In medieval paintings of the crucifixion, you can sometimes see angels reverently catching Christ's blood in communion cups to use at Mass. The pelican was seen as a symbol of Christ because, according to legend, she pierced her breast to feed her young with her blood. During the persecution of early Christians, martyrs who shed their blood were seen as carrying on Christ's saving work. The blood of martyrs poured on the earth was seen as fertile rain which caused the Church to grow. On the feast days of martyrs, red vestments are worn by the priest for Mass.

Blood Rituals

In Europe, goats and lambs are still roasted at Easter for the traditional family meal of celebration. In some places, lambs are still sacrificed in ancient spring-time rituals. In Kirtlington, Oxfordshire at Eastertide, a three-day parade was led by a lamb carried on a man's shoulders until recently. It had to be the finest of the flock, as in the days of ancient Israel, and the firstborn lamb of the season if possible. For three days it was carried round the parish, and admired and reverenced as a sacrificial victim. Then it was slaughtered, cooked and made into pies which were cut up and distributed among the people. In parts of Devon a ram was roasted: in Kingsteignton on Whit Monday a living ram lamb was decorated with flowers and ribbons, and drawn through the village in a cano-pied cart decked with garlands. It was paid honour as a sacrificial victim due to die for the good of the people on the next day. On Whit Tuesday it was killed, and the dressed and decorated carcase was paraded through the streets on a handbarrow, then roasted and carved. Traditionally, everyone was to receive a slice. The roasting still takes place on a spit before a huge open-air fire (Hole 1976, pp.177,246).

Other ceremonies resemble the ancient passover ritual. The Germanic tribes of northern Europe celebrated the beginning of winter and the new year around November 11th, which was the feast of St. Martin of Tours, or Martinmas; Martinmas therefore acquired traditions from pre-Christian new year festivals. At Martinmas it was traditional to slaughter cattle and other animals, since they could not be kept through the winter; most were salted, pickled or dried, and there would be a Martinmas feast. In Ireland until the last century, an animal which varied according to the means of the family was slaughtered on Martin-mas Eve. If it was a sheep or a lamb, the master killed it, and if it was a bird from the poultry yard, his wife killed it. They sprinkled its blood over the house, inside and outside, and over the byre and the rest of the buildings. They made the sign of the cross in blood on both sides of the threshold and on the door, and on the foreheads of the family, including the children. The meat was eaten that night, or on the following day (Hole 1976, pp.190–191). This follows quite closely the passover ritual described in The Book of Exodus: 'The Lord said to Moses and Aaron in the land of Egypt, "this month is to be the first of all others for you… Each man must take an animal from the flock, one for each family: one animal for each household… You may take it from either sheep or goats… The whole assembly of the community of Israel shall slaughter it… Some of the blood must then be taken and put on the two doorposts and the lintel of the houses where it is eaten… The blood shall serve to mark the houses that you live in. When I see the blood I will pass over you and you shall escape the destroying plague when I strike the land of Egypt. This day is to be a day of remembrance for you, and you must celebrate it as a feast in the Lord's honour"' (*Exodus* 12:1–14).

The Blood of Jesus

The concept of sacrifice is a difficult one to grasp, but we do end up sacrificing our lives for one another in various ways, and for Christians the central sacrifice is that of Christ dying on the cross; each Mass is a memorial of this. An early sixteenth century carol describes the sacrifice of the Mass in beautiful imagery: Jesus is a knight who lies bleeding on his bed. The bed is the altar in church, richly hung with brocades. Mary kneels at her son's side, weeping. A stone is inscribed with the words 'Corpus Christi', 'the body of Christ':

> **chorus:** Lully, lulley, lully, lulley!
> The falcon hath born my mate away.

> **verses:** He bore him up, he bore him down,
> He bore him into an orchard brown.

> In that orchard there was an hall
> That was hanged with purple and pall.

> And in that hall there was a bed;
> It was hanged with gold so red.

> And in that bed there lieth a knight,
> His wounds bleeding day and night.

> By that bed's side kneeleth a may,
> And she weepeth both night and day.

> And by that bed's side there standeth a stone;
> 'Corpus Christi' is written thereon.

A version from Derbyshire adds:

> Under that bed there runs a flood:
> The one half runs water, the other runs blood.

At the bed's foot there grows a thorn
Which ever blossoms since he was born.

(Dearmer, Vaughan Williams and Shaw 1928, pp.126–127)

The thorn blossom is a new element introduced from the legend of the holy grail, according to which a thorn bush blossomed in Glastonbury where Joseph of Arimathea planted his staff. In a more important feature of the legend, Joseph used a chalice to catch the blood of Jesus as he died on the cross. He brought the chalice, or holy grail, together with the spear which pierced Christ's side, to England and hid it in a castle ruled over by a wounded king whose land was also desolate. A hero was needed to discover the grail, and so restore life and healing to the land and its king. The legend is part of the Arthurian cycle, but it derives from pre-Christian Celtic sources, in which the grail is sometimes a stone, or a food-bearing dish or a chalice into which a bloodstained spear is thrust. This was the sacrificial dish of the Celtic moon goddess from which one drank to obtain inspiration, regeneration and renewal. It is an age-old symbol of the human search for wholeness, achieved only at great cost.

A fourteenth century woman, Catherine of Siena, forged a personal vision from these themes of life and death and the blood of the lamb. In a vivid piece of writing she describes her work, her life and her death. She feels that when she dies, drowned in the blood of Christ, she will pass into the Pacific Ocean, or 'peaceful sea' of the Godhead. She won't be alone because she will take with her all the people she has helped or saved, her 'troop of lambs', and God will affectionately arrange them in heaven. Here is how she says it. God speaks: 'The good person does not turn his head to admire his past virtues, because he can't and won't hope in his own virtues, but only in the blood in which he has found mercy. He lives in the memory of that blood, and in death he is made drunk with it and drowns in it. Drowned in the blood, passing suddenly through the narrow door of the Word, he reaches me, the Pacific Ocean. You pass through Jesus, the door, drowned in his blood, with your troop of lambs, the many people you have brought to eternal life by your holy words and example, and you leave many behind you living in grace. So they pass through gloriously, bathed in the blood, and by my goodness I arrange each in his place, and give affectionate love to each, as he has given to me'(Catherine of Siena 1925, pp.170–171). The blood of Jesus was an important symbol for many Medieval writers, as it is in revivalist Churches today, but blood is an intense symbol which we can find overpowering. It can be a useful exercise to befriend this symbol and give it some of the positive attributes that it has held for our ancestors through the centuries.

CHAPTER 4

The Snake in Paradise Lost and Regained

The Serpent's Power

The serpent is more widely found in world mythologies than any other creature. It is a powerful symbol, but it can be a difficult one to grasp in Western cultures because we tend to dislike snakes. Ancient peoples saw and used snakes more than we do: in Egypt, people kept house-snakes to kill rats and mice, much as we keep cats today. Snakes exist almost everywhere, in the desert, in water and in woods. In the world of symbol, the serpent represents pure energy, probably because of its sinuous movement. Although we think of snakes as evil, in India snakes are regarded as guardians of the springs of life and immortality (Cirlot 1962, pp.285–286). Since the snake represents energy, intertwined snakes stand for positive and negative energies, the negative contained by the positive. Thus the two intertwined snakes of Mercury are a sign of integration and healing. This symbol, the caduceus, is a symbol of doctors and their healing art to this day.

Almost all aboriginal Australian tribes revere Rainbow Serpent. This giant serpent represents water, and lives in deep water holes, where he is often seen as the rainbow in waterfalls. He is the agent and symbol of fertility, and is often brightly painted with a red head. He embodies the creative and destructive power of nature as it is experienced through rain and through all other waters. Rainbow Serpent makes the tides ebb and flow, and brings spirit-children into the clan waterholes in the Kimberleys. He made rivers all over the continent by his motion while capturing or escaping from enemies; when he was angry, he ate whole camps of people. Rainbow Serpent causes the changing seasons, the growth, flowering and fruiting of plants, and makes animals and people multiply (McCarthy 1957, p.129).

The Snake Coiled Round the Tree of Life

The snake of the Greek and Roman god of healing was a tree snake; it appears coiled around the staff of the healing god. Similarly, a snake coiled round a tree

12. **Rainbow Serpent giving birth to aboriginal people.** (From a bark painting, Arnhem Land, Australia, in the Pitt Rivers Museum, Oxford)

13. *Asclepius, the Greek god of healing, with a snake coiled round his staff.* (Drawing by Steven Nemethy, from a statue in Epidauros Museum)

trunk appears in the rites of the ancient Babylonian goddess of fertility, Ishtar, (known as Astarte by the Canaanites), a goddess familiar to the ancient Israelites. The tree was a female symbol of growth, and the snake signified fertility. The snake encircling a tree trunk became the serpent coiled round the tree of life in the garden of Eden. In Israelite mythology, Eden or paradise was a garden planted by God, with luscious vegetation, including a tree of life, and a tree of knowledge of good and evil. A spring rising in the garden flowed into the four great rivers of the known world, and God put the first people in the garden to enjoy it. The name 'Eden' is possibly Babylonian, while 'paradise' is a Persian word describing an enclosure such as a royal park or hunting ground, which is made more beautiful than its surroundings by cultivation. When the Old Testament was translated into Greek in the third century BC, its translators used the word paradise with this meaning, for example, in words put into Solomon's mouth: 'I made myself gardens and parks, and I planted in them all kinds of fruit trees' (*Ecclesiastes* 2:5) (Warner 1970, p.49).

The tree of life in the middle of the garden, round which the serpent was coiled, did not become an apple tree until early Christian times, when the story of the golden apples of the Hesperides had become famous in Greece and Rome. One of the labours of Hercules was to slay the serpent Ladon who was twined round an apple tree in the garden of the Hesperides (or 'daughters of evening') on which golden apples grew. According to the author of *Genesis*, the snake was originally coiled round the tree in upright posture, its energy directed towards God. When God cursed the snake in the words, 'you shall crawl on your belly and eat dust all the days of your life' (*Genesis* 3:14), it became a symbol of negative energy, or energy run wild, as it crawled in horizontal position, its energy diffused along the ground, no longer focused on God.

The spinal cord of a person resembles a vertical snake; that of an animal resembles a horizontal snake. In the fresco by Michelangelo on the Sistine Chapel ceiling, and in many earlier paintings, the snake in the garden of Eden is portrayed as an upright figure with a human head. Coiled around the tree of life, it engages Adam and Eve in conversation. Since the snake symbolises both positive and negative energy, it also represents temptation, our struggle to cope with both positive and negative forces. Adam and Eve were enjoying the good life of paradise, and in order to grow into a new state of awareness they had to pass through the serpent's temptation, learning to deal with positive and negative energy. This is symbolised in the story of the tree of knowledge of good and evil.

The Healing Serpent

Good and bad serpents reappear in the story of the Israelite runaway slaves trekking through the desert towards their promised land. They became hungry and thirsty and complained to God, who punished them with poisonous snake bites. Moses intervened, and God instructed him to make a bronze serpent coiled round a pole, the symbol of life and healing familiar to ancient Near Eastern peoples. The sick gazed on it and were healed. The book of *Numbers* tells the story (21:4–9): 'The Israelites left Mount Hor by the road to the Sea of Suph (i.e. toward the Gulf of Aqaba). On the way the people lost patience. They spoke against God and against Moses, "Why did you bring us out of Egypt to die in this wilderness? For there is neither bread nor water here; we are sick of this unsatisfying food." At this, God sent fiery serpents among the people; their bite brought death to many in Israel. The people came and said to Moses, "We have sinned by speaking against the Lord and against you. Intercede for us with the Lord to save us from these serpents." Moses interceded for the people, and the Lord answered him, "Make a metal serpent and put it on a pole; if anyone is bitten and looks at it, he shall live." So Moses fashioned a bronze serpent and put it on a pole, and if anyone was bitten by a serpent, he looked at the bronze serpent and lived'.

Jesus used this powerful symbol to describe his healing death which would render powerless the poison of sin. Raised high on the tree of the cross, he would bring life to all who gazed on him. John the Evangelist has Jesus explaining to Nicodemus:

> The Son of Man must be lifted up
> as Moses lifted up the serpent in the desert,
> so that everyone who believes
> may have eternal life in him (*John* 3:13–15).

According to the evangelist, Jesus longed for this to happen, and just before his death he repeated:

> When I am lifted up from the earth
> I shall draw all men to myself

John adds: 'By these words he indicated the kind of death he would die' (*John* 12:32–33).

14. *Moses erects a bronze serpent in the desert.* *(Drawing by Steven Nemethy from an 11th centry bronze door, St Zeno's, Verona)*

In early medieval paintings of the crucifixion, especially those of the Sienese school, Jesus hangs in snake-like posture on the cross. In a redemptive movement he absorbs the negative energy of the world, raising it towards God as positive energy. His action reverses that of the serpent in the garden of Eden. In later art, his mother Mary is understood to help him in his redeeming work, and is portrayed standing upon the serpent of Eden. This refers to the words of God to Eve and the serpent in the Genesis story:

> I will make you enemies of each other:
> you and the woman,
> your offspring and her offspring.
> It (*i.e. her child*) will crush your head
> and you will strike its heel (*Genesis* 3:15).

In some Counter-Reformation paintings of the crucifixion, a snake with an apple in its mouth appears at the foot of the cross; thus positive and negative energy is held in balance in one of nature's most powerful symbols.

Satan, the Evil Serpent
Since the serpent is such an ambivalent symbol, it has attracted much negative energy in Christian thought. The Latin word for serpent is 'draco', and the same

word means 'dragon'. This opens out into a world of sea monsters ('leviathan') and devils. The image of evil as a composite, animal-like creature is found in Egyptian and Persian religions, and from this source came the many-headed monsters in the New Testament book of *Revelation*. In medieval Christian art, the monster became human, but kept some beast-like qualities: claws instead of hands and feet, a tail, and sometimes wings. The wings remind us that Satan, the evil dragon, or 'primeval serpent', started life as an angel, for the Church taught that Satan fell from heaven before people were created. Satan was also called Lucifer (Latin for 'morning star'), quoting a phrase from the prophet Isaiah: 'How have you fallen from heaven, bright morning star?' (*Isaiah* 14:12). In medieval paintings the rebel angels tumble from heaven, acquiring tails and claws as they fall. At the bottom lies Satan, perhaps in the mouth of Leviathan, the sea monster. At the top, in heaven, angels defend God with lances (Hall 1974, p.285). The book of *Revelation* describes the 'war which broke out in heaven' and the dragon, Satan, is often painted being slain by God's chief archangel, Michael.

Medieval writers have left us graphic descriptions of Satan as they imagined him from dreams and visions. Julian of Norwich, writing in the fourteenth century, describes a rather shapeless fiend who tried to strangle her with its paws: 'In my sleep, at the beginning, I thought the fiend had me by the throat, putting his face very near mine. It was like a young man's face, and long and extraordinarily lean: I never saw the like. The colour was the red of a tilestone newly fired, and there were black spots like freckles, dirtier than the tilestone. His hair was rust red, clipped in front, with sidelocks hanging over his cheeks. He grinned at me with sly grimace, thereby revealing white teeth, which made it, I thought, all the more horrible. There was no proper shape to his body or hands, but with his paws he held me by the throat and would have strangled me if he could... I knew that it was the fiend who had come to torment me'(Julian of Norwich 1966, p.182).

Dragons

The evil dragon Satan, and indeed other dragons, vary in appearance, and are often a mixture of several creatures. One of the earliest dragons, depicted in white glaze against a blue background on a gate in ancient Babylon, has a ram's head and horns, a lion's forelegs, a scaly, reptilian body and tail, and the hind legs of an eagle. The ancient Egyptian dragon was closer to the crocodile in shape, since Egyptians were familiar with this beast lurking in the Nile. Dragons are dangerous with their forked tongue and tail, glaring eyes and flared nostrils and their scorching breath. Their sharp teeth and claws and armour-plated bodies show their dangerous power. Their primeval element is not fire but water: they are often found in relation to the sea, rivers, lakes, water spouts or rain clouds. Although they are dangerous, the ambivalence of the serpent is found in them too: in the East, the dragon is a symbol of prosperity, and there are many tales of acts of kindness performed by dragons. Often they guard a treasure which a hero struggles to capture (Warner 1970, p.213).

In Canaanite myths, leviathan was the primordial dragon; he was a monster of the deep, who symbolised the turbulent waters. In creation myths of the ancient Near East, the creator god overcame leviathan, a many-headed monster who represented the primeval waters of chaos; the creator was then able to establish world order. One of the psalms describes God's creative power thus:

> It was you who split the sea by your power;
> you broke the heads of the monster in the waters.
> It was you who crushed the heads of leviathan
> and gave him as food to the creatures of the desert
> (*Psalm* 74:13–14).

The author of the book of *Job* describes leviathan as a terrible crocodile-like animal, closer in shape to the dragon of ancient Egypt. Towards the end of the book, God reminds Job of his limited powers and asks him:

> Can you pull in the leviathan with a fishhook
> or tie down his tongue with a rope?
> Can you put a cord through his nose
> or pierce his jaw with a hook?...
> Can you fill his hide with harpoons
> Or his head with fishing spears?
> If you lay a hand on him,
> you will remember the struggle and never do it again!...
> His snorting throws out flashes of light;
> his eyes are like the rays of dawn.
> Firebrands stream from his mouth,
> sparks of fire shoot out.
> Smoke pours from his nostrils...
> and flames dart from his mouth...
> Nothing on earth is his equal—
> a creature without fear (*Job* 41:1–34).

The prophet Isaiah speaks of a final day of judgement, when God will slay leviathan:

> In that day,
> the Lord will punish with his sword,
> his fierce, great and powerful sword,
> leviathan the gliding serpent,
> leviathan the coiling serpent;
> he will slay the monster of the sea (*Isaiah* 27:1).

In the first century AD, the author of the book of *Revelation* takes up this theme. The dragon tries to devour the young Christian community, but on the last day God will overpower him. This time he is a many-headed red dragon, who derives from Set-Typhon, the red crocodile of Egyptian mythology. He is a huge red dragon with 'seven heads and ten horns, and each of the seven heads crowned with a coronet. His tail dragged a third of the stars from the sky and dropped them to the earth' (*Revelation* 12:3–4). Being a water serpent, he tries to drown the young community, represented here by a young mother: 'The serpent vomited water from his mouth, like a river, after the woman, to sweep her away in the current, but the earth came to her rescue; it opened its mouth and swallowed the river thrown up by the dragon's jaws' (*Revelation* 12:15–16). Finally, God's angel overpowers the dragon: 'I saw an angel come down from heaven with the key of the abyss in his hand and an enormous chain. He over-powered the dragon, that

15. *St. George slays a dragon resembling a crocodile, from the Bruges Garter Book, c. 1430. (Drawing by Margaret Rees)*

primeval serpent which is the devil and Satan, and chained him up for a thousand years. He threw him into the abyss, and shut the entrance and sealed it over him' (*Revelation* 20:1–3).

To early Christians, a dragon often symbolised the evil of paganism, particularly if the pagans concerned were trying to kill Christians. An artist would symbolically depict the conversion of a heathen country to Christianity by portraying the missionary saint slaying a dragon with a spear. This is how St. George emerged. Early paintings show him winning Cappadocia for the faith, the place being represented, according to convention, by a young woman. Later paintings of St. George have lost this meaning; their artists rework the images in terms of the stories familiar to them from classical antiquity. Thus the thirteenth century Golden Legend describes St. George, like Perseus, fighting a dragon by the seashore, outside the city walls, in order to rescue the king's daughter, who is about to be offered as a sacrifice. In art of this period, St. George is dressed in armour, and often mounted on a white horse as a symbol of his purity. The dragon is a scaly, winged monster, often with a snake's forked tongue and a tail.

16. *A buck-toothed St George pierces the dragon's heart, from a 17th century Ethiopian gospel book in the British Library. (Drawing by Margaret Rees)*

The Ambivalent Power of Animals

How did animals come to symbolise good on the one hand and evil on the other? Probably by a natural process of polarisation. Animals represent instinctive energy, which can be lifegiving or destructive. A bull provides nourishing meat, but an angry bull can gore a person to death. Since bulls seemed to have almost godlike power, one of the Babylonian gods was a bull, and the Egyptian goddess Hathor was cow-headed. The prophet Ezekiel had a vision of God sitting on a throne borne up by creatures with the faces of a bull, a lion, an eagle and a man (*Ezekiel* 1:1–26), and in Christian times these became symbols of the four evangelists. In these examples, animals represent awe-inspiring power, though such power can equally be terrifying and destructive. The prophet Daniel saw a vision of four huge beasts emerging from a raging ocean: a winged lion, a rampant bear chewing human flesh, a four-headed leopard and a bull-like horned beast with iron teeth (*Daniel* 7:2–10). In this vision we are made aware of the destruction that animals can wreak.

Like bulls, sheep and goats gave life to their owners, and so were offered to God in sacrifice, but equally they could symbolise uncontrolled, destructive power. Daniel had a vision of a giant ram locked in combat with a goat whose horns grew strong enough to attack the army of heaven, the stars themselves', and which went on to attack God and desecrate his temple (*Daniel* 8:1–14). Dragons were normally composite animals with the combined power of various beasts while, on the other hand, Near Eastern temples were guarded by similar composite animals whose energy was harnessed to protect the holy. Christ was born between an ox and an ass, a reminder, perhaps, that the foundation of human nature is animal instinct to be tamed, healed and befriended.

Because animals can represent untamed instinct, Christian leaders were vigorous in condemning animal rituals, and animals easily became associated with evil. Their primary presence, however, is lifegiving: they give us meat and drink. Their God-given fertility was of vital importance, especially to herding peoples of the Near East. The author of *Genesis* describes God bringing animals into existence by a creative word: 'Then God commanded, "Let the earth produce all kinds of animal life: domestic and wild, large and small", and it was done. So God made them all, and he was pleased with what he saw' (*Genesis* 1:24). And although Christianity has remained ambivalent towards animals and their power, ceremonies with animals have taken place from earliest times until the present day, even in well-Christianised countries.

Animal Rituals

Animals appear in ancient works of religious art. Animal paintings are found on the walls of caves in France, Spain, Scandinavia and Africa dating back to the last Ice Age (between 60,000 and 10,000 BC). In the fifteenth century AD, Pope Calixtus II forbade religious ceremonies in 'caves with horse-pictures', and passing nomads still lay their votive offerings before the old rock paintings in North Africa. These caves were religious places, often approached through low, dark passages to protect their mystery. Most palaeolithic cave paintings are of animals, whose movements and postures have been depicted very skilfully. Some paintings were apparently used as targets, as prayers for food by hunters. Others show animals mating, and seem to have been the focus of prayers for their fertility. A male and female bison are shown mating in the Tuc d'Audubert cave in France (Jaffé 1964, pp.234–235). In the Trois Frères cave in France, a man wrapped in animal hide plays a flute to charm the animals, and another painting in the cave represents a dancing person with antlers, a horse's head and bears' paws. He is surrounded by several hundred animals, and appears to be 'Lord of the animals'. Today in societies close to nature, the tribal chief still appears at initiation ceremonies disguised as an animal. He becomes the animal spirit, a terrifying demon who will circumcise the young men. He represents the ancestor of the tribe and, ultimately, the primal god (Jaffé 1964, pp.235–236).

Going around in animal disguises at important seasons such as the winter festival was a pagan practice which Christian church leaders tried to suppress, since they saw it as 'dabbling with the devil', the primeval monster. In the fifth century Caesarius of Arles wrote: 'The heathen and, what is worse, some who have been baptised, put on counterfeit forms and monstrous faces... Some are clothed in the hides of cattle; others put on the heads of beasts, rejoicing and exulting that they have so transformed themselves into the shapes of animals that they no longer appear to be men'. The ninth century Penitential of Pseudo-Theodore states: 'If anyone at the Kalends of January goes about as a stag or a bull, that is, making himself into a wild animal, and putting on the heads of beasts; those who in such wise transform themselves into the appearance of a wild animal, (must do) penance for three years, because this is devilish'. However, people continued to do so all over Europe, including Britain, until this century (Hole 1976, p.65).

One of these animals was the Christmas bull, known in Dorset, Wiltshire and Gloucestershire. He was a man wearing a hollowed-out bull's head with horns and glass eyes, or else he supported the bull's head on a pole above his own head so that he seemed to be wearing it. In Dorset he went round the parish at Christmas, usually at dusk, with a keeper and a band of men. He was allowed into any room of any house, and everyone fled at his approach. The horse still visits many areas, as a bringer of fertility. In parts of Wales he is known as the Wassail, probably from the Anglo-Saxon blessing: 'Be whole!'. He brought happiness for the coming year, and before the visitors left they would sing a Welsh verse meaning:

> Farewell, gentle folk,
> We have been made welcome.
> God's blessing be upon your house,
> And upon all who dwell there (Hole 1976, pp.186–187).

The horn dance at Abbots Bromley in Staffordshire was originally a winter solstice custom, and seems to be a pre-Christian ritual associated with either hunting or fertility. Six dancers carry pairs of ancient reindeer antlers so that they appear to be springing from their heads, and accompanying them are a man dressed as a woman (now called Maid Marian), a fool, a hobby horse, a bowman and a musician who once played a pipe and tabor. They spend the whole day travelling round the 20-mile parish dancing in front of farms and cottages. After their fortune-bringing visits, they spend the evening feasting (Hole 1976, pp.152–154).

On May Day, the hobby horses of Padstow and Minehead come out to meet the summer. In Padstow the horse gambols through the streets, chasing the girls; if he corners one against a wall, he covers her with his huge tarpaulin skirt to bring her a husband within a year or, if she already has one, a baby. Besides bringing fertility, he appears to have brought rain, for he used to go to a pool and drink from it, after which his spectators were sprinkled with water. Every now and then, the horse 'dies'. He sinks to the ground and his 'club man' gently strokes his head with his club, while onlookers sing his dirge. Then the music changes again, and the horse leaps up, full of life. He has brought back summer's life again (Hole 1976, pp.199–201). In east Kent, the Hooden Horse falls ill, dies and is restored to life in a yearly ritual. These are ceremonies which were never christianised, but which express a basic human belief in the goodness of life and fertility.

In Paradise, Animals Live at Peace

If animals have been ambivalent symbols in the past, visionaries have often seen a future when their negative and positive energies will be held in perfect balance. In the eighth century BC, the prophet Isaiah spoke of a future day when animals will live at peace because integrity and justice will reign. All will live together on God's holy mountain:

> Wolves and sheep will live together in peace,
> and leopards will lie down with young goats.
> Calves and lion cubs will feed together,
> and little children will take care of them.
> Cows and bears will eat together,
> and their calves and cubs will lie down in peace.
> Lions will eat straw as cattle do.
> Even the baby will not be harmed
> if it plays near a poisonous snake (*Isaiah* 11:6–8).

Writing at the same time though from a different culture, Virgil describes a similar scene in his *Eclogues*.

Isaiah based his vision of future peace on his people's stories of how things began. According to the book of *Genesis*, God gave Adam and Eve power over the animals, wild and tame, great and small, and God cared for the animals by providing grass and leafy plants in paradise for them to eat, so they would not hunt each other (*Genesis* 1:26–30). The balance of things became upset when Adam and Eve disobeyed God, who then drove the couple out of Eden. In Hebrew mythology, paradise remained an 'otherworld', part of our universe, yet better and happier than the part we know. People once lived there, carefree and guiltless, without sickness or hard work, although now death, disease and wickedness have poisoned life.

This myth of a golden age in another world was shared by other cultures. The ancient Greeks looked to the Isles of the Blest, out over the Atlantic, beyond a barrier of water, where the plain of Elysium was to be found at the world's end. Homer described it as a place where 'living is made easiest for mankind, no snow falls, no strong winds blow and there is never any rain'. Gods lived there, and they were joined by a few noble humans who were awarded immortality as a special gift. The Greek concept of Elysium began to change in the sixth century BC when mystics of the cult of Orpheus proclaimed salvation as a release from matter and from earthly bondage. The Elysian fields now became a bright otherworld, a happy resting place for pure spirits of initiates who had lived well. Later Greek cults began to think of this good place as being up in the sky. Purified souls would soar to a heaven beyond our planetary system where they would live in happiness with the gods and other good souls for ever (Warner 1970, pp.49–51).

The Kingdom of Heaven

Meanwhile, Hebrew tradition was developing differently. Until the sixth century BC, the Hebrew paradise was a lost garden, and there was no clear notion of immortality. Heaven meant the sky, beyond which was a divine heaven where God sat enthroned among his angels. After the Israelites returned from exile in the sixth century BC, they developed more positive beliefs. Cyrus, King of Persia, allowed the Jews to return to their homeland, and it was probably under the influence of Persian Zoroastrian beliefs that Israelites began to think of a future resurrection of the dead, a last judgement and a world to come, which would be a paradise on earth. In the time of Jesus, this crystallised in their hopes for a Messiah. The Lord's anointed one would appear, life would be trans-figured, the dead would rise and the earthly kingdom would become paradise (Warner 1970, p.52). The book of *Revelation* describes a final judgement and a material new Jerusalem for resurrected saints.

Christianity combined Greek and Hebrew concepts of heaven. Early Chris-tians believed that heaven must already be accessible, for when Jesus was dying on the cross he promised the good thief: 'This day you will be with me in paradise' (*Luke* 23:43). Christians conceived of a rather Greek journey of souls through the seven heavens until they reached the home of God beyond the cosmic system. However, Christians also took up the rather different Hebrew concept of a last judgement, after which heaven would appear on earth. Medie-val Christians did not really decide whether judgement and bliss happened at death or at the end of the world. St. Augustine attempted to resolve the question by suggesting an interim life in heaven until the end of the world, a foretaste of things to come (Warner 1970, pp.52–53).

But if Christian thinkers were not sure about the heavenly time sequence, they were clear that there would be an end to chaos, dragons and sea serpents. Leviathan was to be driven firmly down into the abyss, and the sea monster would have no place in which to exist, for the author of the book of *Revelation* declared that with the coming of the new heaven and the new earth, the old earth would pass away, and there would be no more sea (*Revelation* 21:2). Since leviathan was the turbulent sea at the dawn of creation in bodily form, he was thereby declared redundant, and joined the dinosaurs as remote memories of a distant past.

CHAPTER 5

The Tree of Life
and the Tree of the Cross

In 1784, one Joshua Smith of New Hampshire recorded a song which was sung by American settlers, entitled 'Jesus Christ the apple tree'. It describes the tree of life which provides apples for food, in whose shade one can rest after a hot day's work. It runs:

> The tree of life my soul hath seen,
> Laden with fruit, and always green:
> The trees of nature fruitless be
> Compared with Christ the apple tree.
>
> His beauty doth all things excel:
> By faith I know, but ne'er can tell
> The glory which I now can see
> In Jesus Christ the apple tree.
>
> For happiness I long have sought
> And pleasure dearly have I bought:
> I missed of all; but now I see
> 'Tis found in Christ the apple tree.
>
> I'm weary with my former toil,
> Here I will sit and rest awhile:
> Under the shadow I will be
> Of Jesus Christ the apple tree.
>
> This fruit doth make my soul to thrive,
> It keeps my dying faith alive;
> Which makes my soul in haste to be
> With Jesus Christ the apple tree.
>   (Holbrook and Poston 1967, no.111, p.168)

The World-Axis Tree

The tree is a powerful symbol of the life of the cosmos, representing its growth and proliferation, its continual birth and rebirth. Since it symbolises inexhaustible life, it also stands for immortality. From pre-Neolithic times the tree was seen as the world-axis: its long shape makes it an axis to the centre of the world. Since each tree is an axis to the world's centre, there can be many holy trees. With its roots in the ground and its branches in the sky, the tree connects the underworld, earth and the heavens, with its roots, trunk and foliage. Since the tree symbolises immortality, there was a tree of life in the garden of Eden. It stood in the middle of the garden, since it was an axis to the world's centre. Coiled around it was its guardian snake. The scene at the crucifixion of Christ resembled the scene in the garden of Eden: the tree of life grew in the garden of Eden and in the garden of Calvary. Medieval tradition explained how the wood of the cross came from the original tree of life in Eden. Like all holy trees, the tree of the cross is an axis to the centre of the world, its roots reaching back to the beginning of time; because of this, Adam's skull is sometimes portrayed at the base of the cross (Cirlot 1962, p.347).

Archaic peoples worshipped trees as the homes of spirits, and trees were regarded as sources of wisdom. Oracular trees are recorded in Persia, Armenia and Arabia, and in the Old Testament too. When King David was uncertain when to attack the Philistines, balsam trees gave him a signal from the Lord (2 *Samuel* 5:22–25). The oak was considered a holy tree in the Near East and in Europe because it was strong, durable and long-lived. Several stories of the patriarchs indicate that oaks were important to the earliest Hebrew worshippers of God. God appeared to Abraham at Shechem's holy place, the Oak of Moreh (or 'The Revealer'). Here God revealed to him: 'It is to your descendants that I will give this land', and Abraham built an altar beside the oak (*Genesis* 12:6–8). Later, God appeared to Abraham at the oak of Mamre, in the guise of three strangers who promised he would have a son within the year. He made his heavenly visitors an offering of bread, milk and meat under the tree (*Genesis* 18:1–10). Abraham's grandson Jacob buried his household's 'foreign gods' and earrings under the oak of Shechem, where God first offered the land to his grandfather (*Genesis* 35:1–5). Later, when the Israelite tribes tried to conquer the new land, the 'Diviners' Oak' at Shechem again features (*Judges* 9:37).

The Fruitful Tree

Through its annual dying and rebirth, the tree became a symbol of the earth's fertility. In the Near East it was connected with worship of the earth goddess Astarte, and the tree also became a symbol of fertility and fruitfulness for the Israelites. The prophet Hosea (8th century BC) has God say to his people Israel:

> I will fall like dew on Israel
> He shall bloom like the lily,
> and thrust out roots like the poplar,
> his shoots will spread far;
> he will have the beauty of the olive
> and the fragrance of Lebanon.

> They will come back to live in my shade;
> they will grow corn that flourishes,
> they will cultivate vines
> as renowned as the wine of Helbon...
> I am like a cypress ever green,
> all your fruitfulness comes from me' (*Hosea* 14:6–9).

Some trees are less lifegiving than others. Jesus reminded his followers that they could tell a good tree by its fruit, and asked them: 'Can you pick grapes from brambles, or figs from thistles?' (*Matthew* 7:16). Ancient Israelites were equally sensitive to the worth of their trees, and used them to tell stories of human worth. In the book of *Judges*, a wise Israelite named Jotham commented on the election of a bad king by declaring that his people had just chosen a thorn bush instead of a fruit tree. He did this by climbing to the top of their holy mountain, Mount Gerizim, and solemnly chanting this story to them:

> Jotham shouted aloud for them to hear: 'Hear me, leaders of Shechem, that God may also hear you! One day the trees went out to anoint a king to rule over them. They said to the olive tree, "Be our king!" The olive tree answered them, "Must I forego my oil which gives honour to gods and men, to stand swaying above the trees?" Then the trees said to the fig tree, "Come now, you be our king!" The fig tree answered them, "Must I forego my sweetness, forego my excellent fruit, to stand swaying above the trees?" Then the trees said to the vine, "Come now, you be our king!" The vine answered them, "Must I forego my wine which cheers the hearts of gods and men, to stand swaying above the trees?" Then all the trees said to the thorn bush, "Come now, you be our king!" And the thorn bush answered the trees, "If in all good faith you anoint me king to reign over you, then come and shelter in my shade. If not, fire will come from the thorn bush and devour the cedars of Lebanon!"' (*Judges* 9: 7–15).

In this interesting parable, the real riches of the olive, the fig and the vine are contrasted with the sham bravado of the thorn bush, who has no fruit to offer his friends.

People as Trees

We are related in symbol to trees. While animals stand in a horizontal position, we stand vertically, with limbs and a trunk like trees. We are rooted in the earth of our humanity, with the sap of life flowing through us, growing tall, healthy and fruitful as do trees. The ancient Israelite prayers of the psalms have a variety of images for this. The healthy person

> is like a tree that is planted
> by water streams,
> yielding its fruit in season,
> its leaves never fading (*Psalm* 1:3).

If you fear the Lord,

> Happiness and prosperity will be yours.
> Your wife: a fruitful vine
> on the inner walls of your house.
> Your children: around your table
> like shoots around an olive tree (*Psalm* 128:2–3).

Those who are just

> flourish like palm trees
> and grows tall as the cedars of Lebanon.
> Planted in the house of the Lord,
> they will flourish in the courts of our God,
> still bearing fruit in old age,
> still full of sap, still green' (*Psalm* 92:12–14).

The Vine of God

The tree was a symbol for the whole nation too. The ancient Israelites saw themselves as God's fruitful vine. When things went well for Israel, God was tending his vine; when things went badly, God had stopped tending it. One of the psalms laments:

> There was a vine: you uprooted it from Egypt;
> to plant it, you drove out other nations,
> you cleared a space where it could grow.
> it took root and filled the whole country.
> It covered the mountains with its shade,
> the cedars of God with its branches;
> its tendrils extended to the sea,
> its offshoots all the way to the river (Euphrates).
> Why have you destroyed its fences?
> Now anyone can go and steal its grapes;
> the forest boar can ravage it
> and wild animals eat it.
> Please, Lord of hosts, relent!
> Look down from heaven, look at this vine, visit it,
> protect what your own right hand has planted (*Psalm* 80:8–15).

In St. John's gospel Jesus describes himself as the true vine. His faithful followers are his fruitful branches:

> I am the true vine, and my Father is the vinedresser.
> Every branch in me that bears no fruit he cuts away,
> and every branch that does bear fruit he prunes
> to make it bear even more...
> I am the vine, you are the branches.
> Whoever remains in me, with me in him,
> bears fruit in plenty' (*John* 15:1–5).

In ancient cultures, a grove of trees was considered to be a holy place where one could encounter the divine; God walked with Adam among the trees in the garden of Eden (*Genesis* 3:9). Later, temples were built rather like artificial groves, consisting of a space enclosed by pillars made of tree trunks. Ancient Greek temple columns were made of stone, but their fluted columns echoed the grain of tree bark, and their capitals were decorated with carved foliage. Romanesque cathedrals adopted a similar design of stone columns topped with capitals of carved leaves and branches. In later medieval churches, stone branches become fan vaulting as they intertwine across the ribbed roof.

The Tree of the Cross

In many cultures, the concept of a cosmic tree appears. The emperor Charlemagne destroyed a cosmic tree trunk, the Saxon world-pillar named Irmensul. In Nordic myth, the ash Yggdrasil was a tree whose branches spread over the world and reached the heavens; its roots penetrated the abyss. Halfway up its trunk was situated the disc-shaped earth, surrounded by the ocean. A world tree in Indian mythology is the fig tree, Arvattha (Warner 1970, pp.234–236). For Christians, the cross is the cosmic world tree, and early Christians found many images to remind them of it, as their iconography shows, from the plough and the ship's mast crossed by a spar, to a bird in flight and the shape of the human person with hands outstretched in prayer (Rahner 1963, p.55).

Since crucifixion was a normal form of death for Roman criminals, early martyrs suffered it as their master had, and a theology of the cross developed as writers attempted to record the feelings of dying martyrs about their crucifixion. A third century account of the death of the apostle Andrew describes how he was taken to the sea shore, where he was crucified: 'And he went to the cross and spoke loudly to it, as if it were alive: "Hail, O cross! Yes, be truly glad! I know well that I shall soon be at rest, and that you have been weary for a long time, set up and waiting for me. I come to you, whom I know to belong to me. I come to you who have yearned after me...O cross, trophy of the victory of Christ over the enemies! O cross, planted in the earth, with your fruit in the heavens!...But how long do I delay, speaking in this way, rather than embrace the cross, so that I may be made alive by the cross, and by it win the common death of all, and depart from life?" Andrew then calls the king's executioners to do their task: "Come here to me, you ministers of joy, you servants of Aegeates. Fulfil the desire of us both, and bind the lamb to the wood of suffering, man to his maker, and the soul to its saviour..." And when blessed Andrew had finished speaking, he stood and gazed on the cross, and told the brothers to call the executioners to come and do what they had been commanded, for they stood at a distance. And they came and bound his hands and feet... And they left him hanging there, and went away' (Rhodes James 1924, pp.359–360).

Andrew's cross took its meaning from the cross of Christ. Throughout the early Church at Eastertime, bishops preached to their flock about the mystery of the cross. In a third century Easter sermon, Hippolytus of Rome wrote: 'This tree, wide as the heavens itself, has grown up into heaven from earth. It is an immortal growth, and towers between heaven and earth' Hippolytus continues to describe this cosmic tree of life: 'It is the fulcrum of all things, and the place where they are at rest. It is the foundation of the round world, the centre of the cosmos. In it all the diversities in our human nature are formed into a unity. It is held together by invisible nails of the Spirit so that it may not break loose from the divine. It touches the highest summits of heaven and makes the earth firm beneath its foot, and it grasps the middle regions between them with its immeasurable arms' (*Hippolytus: De Pascha Homilia 6* in Rahner 1963 (i), p.67).

The Easter Candle

During Eastertime, a huge candle was set on a stand in every church. The candle represented the light of the risen Christ, and was solemnly lit from a new fire on Easter night. The basilica of St. Paul's outside the Walls in Rome possesses an Easter candle stand some ten feet high which was carved around 1180 AD, inscribed with words describing its function:

> A tree bears fruit.
> I am a tree, but I bear light.
> Christ is risen.
> Such is the gift I bring (Rahner 1963 (i), p.83).

From the third century, the Easter candle has continued to symbolise the crucified Christ. It is made from pure beeswax, and marked with a cross, the year (and hence the number of years of redemption), and the first and last letters of the Greek alphabet, to symbolise Christ as the beginning and end of all life. Into the candle five large grains of incense are inserted, to represent the five wounds of the risen, glorious Saviour. Since the Easter candle is also seen as a tree of life, it is lavishly decorated with flowers. Its fruit is its light, the risen Jesus.

Medieval Christians developed a tender devotion to the cross as the tree of life. During the Good Friday liturgy which commemorates the death of Jesus, this hymn was, and still is, sung in its praise:

> Faithful cross! Above all other,
> one and only noble tree!
> None in foliage, none in blossom,
> none in fruit thy peer may be;
> dearest wood and dearest iron!
> Dearest weight is hung on thee...
> Bend thy boughs, O tree of glory!
> Thy relaxing sinews bend;

for a while the ancient rigour
that thy birth bestowed, suspend;
and the King of heavenly beauty
on thy bosom gently tend… (Winstone 1975, pp.202-203)

It is a touching poem, its author asking the cross to carry its human burden
gently.

The Maypole

The tree of life survived in forms other than the cross. In Britain, the tree of life
became the maypole, an ancient fertility symbol which marked the beginning
of summer's new life. Before sunrise on May morning, young people went into
the woods and cut down a tall, young tree, lopping off most of its branches
except for a few at the top. They brought it back to the village green, decorated
it with garlands and flowers, and set it up as an axis point for their dances. The
Puritan Stubbes described how in some parishes, twenty or forty yoke of oxen
dragged it in, 'every ox having a sweet nosegay of flowers tied on the tip of his

17. **Raising the maypole. The maypole is our English axis-tree.** *(From an old print)*

horns, and these oxen draw home this maypole (this stinking idol, rather), which is covered all over with flowers and herbs'. When it was set in place, the villagers began to 'leap and dance about it, as the heathen people did'. Some parishes had a standing maypole, a permanent shaft which remained in position all year, and was newly painted and decorated each May Day. Its normal life-span is about fifteen years, after which its base starts to rot and it has to be renewed. Permanent poles are usually very tall: true axis trees. The pole at Welford-on-Avon is 70 feet high, and has bright red circular stripes. The church of St. Andrew Undershaft in Leadenhall Street, London was so named because the maypole which stood annually beside its south door was taller than the church (Hole 1976, p.205).

An ancient tree-like figure who appears in May is Jack-in-the-Green, Green George, or the Wild Man, who is known all over Europe, and represents summer: he brings in the time of plenty. He is pictured on inn signs in many parts of the country as the Green Man, or the Green King. He appears on May Morning in Oxford, for example, as a man encased in a wickerwork cage, completely covered in green branches, leaves and flowers, with only his feet visible. Sometimes a tree is still venerated as it was long before Christianity. At Aston-le-Clun in Shropshire, the Arbor Tree ceremony takes place on 29th May. The Arbor Tree is a large black poplar in the centre of the village. Once a year it is dressed with flags suspended from long poles, which are fixed to the main branches and left to hang there throughout the year. The ceremony has its roots in ancient tree veneration: this was probably the site of the guardian tree of the early settlement. A similar ceremony called 'bawming the thorn' takes place at Appleton Thorn in Cheshire on about 5th July, old midsummer day. 'Bawming' is a dialect word meaning 'adorning', or perhaps 'balming' or anointing. After a procession through the village, the tree is decorated with flowers, posies, flags and red ribbons, while a song is sung; sports and games follow (Hole 1976, pp.27,32,169).

An ancient spring festival dance to bring in the summer is the Furry Dance at Helston in Cornwall. In this ceremony, green branches are gathered early in the morning and carried about, and dancers bring fertility and blessing into every house. The ancient words of the song the dancers sing explain their purpose:

> For we are up as soon as any day, O,
> And for to fetch the summer home,
> The summer and the May, O,
> For summer is a-come, O
> And winter is a-gone, O.

The Furry Dance is performed on 8th May. Houses and public buildings are decorated with branches of sycamore and beech, flowers and evergreens. The church bells ring, and there is a special early morning service, after which young

18. Mayday celebrations in Charlton-on-Otmoor, Oxfordshire: children taking their flower crosses through the village to the church. Photograph: Margaret Rees

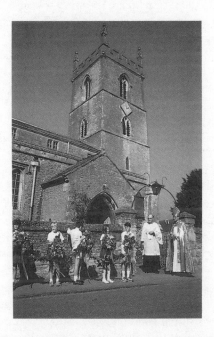

19. Mayday celebrations in Charlton-on-Otmoor, Oxfordshire: the bishop receives the May garland. Photograph: Margaret Rees

people begin the early morning dance at 7am. They wear lilies of the valley, and dance through the narrow streets, and in and out of gardens, houses and shops, if possible in through one door and out through another, to bring the blessings of summer to the owners and drive out the darkness of winter. At noon the main dance begins, led by the mayor, wearing his chain of office. Behind him men and women dance in couples, dressed in their best, through the streets and houses. Later, spectators may join in, until the whole town is dancing (Hole 1976, pp.108–110).

The Blossoming Almond

Fruitful trees originally had strong associations with female earth deities, and in Christian times they became associated with Mary, who bore the Son of God as the fruit of her womb. In medieval art, Mary is frequently represented as an enclosed garden planted with flowers and fruit trees, a symbol of her virginity and fruitfulness. One of her symbols was the almond, a tree sacred to the goddess Astarte before her. When the Israelites were in the desert, a leader was chosen, according to the book of *Numbers*, by a ritual in which the tribal heads each brought a staff to Moses. Next day, the staff of Aaron had sprouted, flowered and produced ripe almonds (*Numbers* 17:1–9). Since 'virga' is Latin for 'staff' and 'virgo' is Latin for 'virgin', the symbol of the unfertilised staff bearing fruit was transferred to the virgin Mary. The story was also adapted to describe her choice of Joseph among her suitors, so Joseph appears in medieval art carrying a blossoming almond wand. The word 'virga' means a staff, rod or shoot; it means 'shoot' in the prophecy of Isaiah: 'A shoot shall grow from the stock of Jesse', the father of King David (*Isaiah* 11:1–3). This was interpreted visually in medieval times in the form of a Jesse tree. This was a genealogical, or family tree of Jesus. The typical 'Jesse window' in stained glass in a medieval church shows Jesse reclining at the foot of the design. A tree rises from his loins, with the ancestors of Christ in its branches; at the top is the virgin Mary and her son (Hall 1974, pp.1,327).

At the beginning of summer, trees are a powerful symbol of abundant life. In midwinter, when most vegetation has withered and died, evergreens flourish and bear fruit, and become symbols of undying life. It was a very ancient custom to bring greenery in to decorate buildings at the midwinter festival and, long before Christianity, evergreens were used in ceremonies to pray for the return of vegetation. Sacred buildings throughout Europe and western Asia were decorated with evergreens for winter solstice ceremonies. Houses were adorned with laurels and bay at the Kalends of January in ancient Rome, and green garlands were given as presents and worn during the week of Saturnalia in December. At first, the Church condemned burning candles at midwinter and fixing laurels to the doorposts. Tertullian wrote: 'If you have renounced temples, do not make a temple of the door of your own house' (Tertullian: *De Idolatria* in

Hole 1976, p.71). This was in the mid-second century, when non-Christian Roman rituals were very widespread, but gradually suspicion softened, and in time, Christian homes and churches became splendidly decorated with greenery at Christmas. In 604, St. Augustine of Canterbury was given permission by Pope Gregory I to use evergreens at Christmas time (Green 1983, p.23).

Holly, Ivy and Mistletoe

From early times, laurel and bay, rosemary, box, fir and pine have been used as decorations, but favourite evergreens have always been holly, ivy and mistletoe, which bear their distinctive fruit in winter. Prickly holly with its bright red berries is traditionally masculine, and trailing ivy feminine. However, in the ancient and widespread carol 'The Holly and the Ivy', the holly represents Mary:

'The holly and the ivy,
when they are both full grown,
of all the trees that are in the wood,
the holly bears the crown.
The rising of the sun
and the running of the deer,
the playing of the merry organ,
sweet singing in the choir.

The holly bears a blossom,
as white as the lily flower,
and Mary bore sweet Jesus Christ
to be our sweet saviour.

The holly bears a berry,
as red as any blood,
and Mary bore sweet Jesus Christ
to do poor sinners good.

The holly bears a prickle
as sharp as any thorn,
and Mary bore sweet Jesus Christ
on Christmas day in the morn.

The holly bears a bark
as bitter as any gall,
and Mary bore sweet Jesus Christ
for to redeem us all.' (Dearmer et al 1928, no.38)

Another carol on the same theme, 'Now the holly bears a berry', comes from Cornwall (Dearmer et al 1928, no.35, pp.74–75).

Mistletoe was a plant of peace and healing, held holy by Celtic druids and Norsemen. As the 'golden bough' this plant had deep significance for ancient peoples, for it represented the light of the sun hidden in the branches of the forest in winter. By winter, the parasite mistletoe hangs on the branches of the oak as a golden, sun-dried fruit (Cirlot 1962, p.212). The mistletoe is a symbol of Christ, the light of the world, born in a hidden way as the sun hides in the forest. Like mistletoe, Christ is the guest of humanity, a tree that did not engender him, and like the wise men we search out this light in the darkness, this hidden gold, this buried treasure. Because of its strong pagan associations, many churches did not allow mistletoe among its decorations, but since mistletoe was a plant of peace, under which enemies had to stop fighting, it was honoured in some churches. In medieval times, a branch of mistletoe was ceremonially laid on the high altar of York Minster on Christmas Eve, and left there for the twelve days of Christmas. So long as it remained there, a universal peace and pardon was proclaimed at the city gates. Mistletoe was placed on the altar of the collegiate church in Wolverhampton, and blessed and distributed to the people. The mistletoe was thought to bring not only peace but also healing. One of its names was 'all heal', and it was held to cure many diseases, nullify poison, prevent misfortune and encourage fertility. Until recently, many families kept a bunch of mistletoe hanging up indoors throughout the year, as protection against evil (Hole 1976, p.81, n.16).

The Yule Log

The Christmas tree became popular only from the seventeenth century, and originated in Germany. It was not the Christmas tree but the Yule log which was the ceremonial tree of Christmas festivities in Britain and throughout Europe. A large log of oak, ash or fruit-tree was felled on Christmas Eve, dragged to the door of the house by cart horses or oxen, and ceremonially laid upon the open hearth. It was often decorated with evergreens, and kindled with a fragment of the previous year's log. In some places, corn and wine or ale were sprinkled over it in blessing before it was lit. The Yule Log was the home counterpart of the communal midwinter fire festival, and both were connected with fertility, continuing life, and preservation from evil, but the Yule log's flame also gave warmth to the family's dead who, in many areas, were believed to return to their homes at Christmas. Once lit, the log burned steadily all day or, in some areas, throughout the twelve days of Christmas, without being extinguished.

The Yule log blazing in the fireplace is a symbol of birth from the womb, and for medieval Christians, of Christ born from Mary's womb. In Germany, the Yule log was called the Christbrand, or Christlotz. In many countries, the family held a simple religious ceremony when they brought the Yule log home. In Provence, the whole family went to fetch it, and they sang a carol round it asking God to bless their women, herds, flocks and crops to make them fruitful. They processed round the kitchen in single file and laid the log in the hearth. The father or the youngest child poured wine over the log, calling down God's blessing on them all as he did so. When the first flame was kindled, the father would cross himself and say: 'Burn the log, O fire!', and the family would then sit down and eat (Hole 1976, pp. 333–335).

Throughout history, people have been highly sensitive to trees and their significance at different times of the year. Various trees were brought into the house at various times of the year to indicate the changing seasons, as different coloured vestments would be used in church. Christmas greenery was taken down at Candlemas, which marks the end of the liturgical Christmas season in early February. A seventeenth century Devonshire vicar, Robert Herrick, described the progression of the year from Candlemas to Whitsun, and the trees appropriate to each season, in his *Hesperides*:

> Down with rosemary and bays,
> Down with mistletoe:
> Instead of holly, now upraise
> The greener box, for show.
>
> The holly hitherto did sway:
> Let box now domineer
> Until the dancing Easter day,
> Or Easter's eve appear.
>
> Then youthful box, which now hath grace
> Your houses to renew,
> Grown old, surrender must his place
> Unto the crispèd yew.
>
> When yew is out, then birch comes in,
> and many flowers beside,
> Both of a fresh and fragrant kin,
> To honour Whitsuntide.
>
> Green rushes then, and sweetest bents (*i.e. flowering grasses*),
> With cooler oaken boughs,
> Come in for comely ornaments,
> To readorn the house.
>
> Thus times do shift; each thing his turn does hold;
> New things succeed, as former things grow old
> (Dearmer *et al* 1928, no.126, p.254).

In an age when we are newly aware of the ecological necessity of making peace with our planet, it is interesting to note how keenly our predecessors observed and valued the natural life around them, sensing the harmony between trees and ourselves as we progress through the changing seasons of life.

CHAPTER 6

Sun and Moon; Fire and Light

Ancient peoples were deeply in awe of the sun and the moon, and much of their religious longing centred on these two great forces. Moon Mother watched over mankind from the sky in ancient Babylon, the near East, Egypt and the Celtic countries (Harding 1971, p.95), while ancient Egyptians portrayed the night-travelling sun boat which paddled them safely to the next world, and all of Rome from Emperor to peasant worshipped the sun. The sun cults of ancient Greece and Rome posed a strong challenge to the new religion of Christianity, but the Church was also able to absorb and integrate the ancient world's awe for the sun and moon in her theology and worship.

Christians were certain that our lives do not depend on the fatefully deter-mined courses of the stars; the sun and moon are immensely powerful, but they are creatures of the unseen God. The Church referred all Greek sun symbolism to her founder Jesus, whom Luke described as 'the dawn which visits us from on high' (*Luke* 1:78) and whom John called 'the true light that enlightens everyone who comes into the world' (*John* 1:9). The prophet Malachi had declared: 'For you the sun of righteousness will shine out with healing in its rays' (*Malachi* 4:2), and in the fourth century, bishop Ambrose spelt this out to his people by explaining that 'as the sun rises daily for all, so the mystical Sun of Righteousness rises for all: he appeared for all, he suffered for all, he rose again for all' (Rahner (i) 1963, p.98).

Jesus, the Light of the World

Christ took over the role of Helios and the earlier sun deities in what seems to have been a deliberate use of sun imagery. He made the magnificent claim:

> I am the light of the world;
> anyone who follows me will not be walking in the dark;
> he will have the light of life (*John* 7:12).

As his death approached, he spoke with more urgency:

> The light will be with you only a little longer now.
> Walk while you have the light,
> or the dark will overtake you;

> he who walks in the dark does not know where he is going.
> While you still have the light,
> believe in the light,
> and you will become children of light…
> I, the light, have come into the world
> so that whoever believes in me
> need not stay in the dark any more' (*John* 12:35–36; 46).

Matthew quotes the prophet Isaiah's description of a saviour who will appear like the rising sun:

> The people that lived in darkness
> have seen a great light;
> on those who dwell in the land and shadow of death
> a light has dawned. (*Isaiah* 9:1 = *Matthew* 4:16).

Matthew later describes how Jesus took his friends up a mountain and revealed himself as the sun in splendour: 'There in their presence he was transfigured; his face shone like the sun and his clothes became white as the light' (*Matthew* 17:2). Good people will shine with the reflected glory of this sun, Matthew explains: 'The virtuous will shine like the sun in the kingdom of their Father' (*Matthew* 13:43).

In the gospel of Mark, Jesus describes how he supersedes the sun and moon, and will appear in the clouds more powerfully than either of them: 'In those days, the sun will be darkened, the moon will lose its brightness… And then they will see the Son of Man coming in the clouds with great power and glory' (*Mark* 13:24–26). The theme of Jesus eclipsing natural light reappears in the accounts of his crucifixion. Eclipses were highly significant portents, which priests and scholars from ancient China onwards took great pains to predict, and such monuments as Stonehenge seem to have been built partly for this purpose. If the darkness at the crucifixion is seen as an eclipse, this does not lessen its power or meaning.

The Church set itself a difficult task when it tried to absorb the sun cults of ancient Greece and Rome. The Greek sun god was Helios (Apollo in Roman myth), who drove his chariot across the sky, son of Zeus (Jupiter in Roman myth), the supreme ruler of the gods. New Christians could not easily forget these mighty deities, and bishops like Ambrose tried hard to help their people integrate their old and new beliefs. In a sermon in Milan cathedral, Ambrose quotes Secundus the Platonist philosopher's praises of the sun: 'O sun, world's eye! Joy of the day! Heaven's beauty! Nature's darling! Creation's jewel.' But Ambrose gives the passage a new slant by adding: 'When you see the sun, think of its Lord! When you marvel at it, praise its maker. If the sun shines so kindly, how lovely must Christ the Sun of Righteousness be!'. Origen, writing in the third century, concluded that the sun and moon could now be considered christianised: 'We are sure that the sun and moon offer their prayers to almighty

God through his only-begotten Son' (Rahner (i) 1963, pp.91–92). Prayers could be christianised too: the Christian prayer 'Kyrie eleison', (Greek for 'Lord have mercy'), was first used in pagan rites honouring the sun god, but the Christian West adopted it, and Pope Gregory the Great 'baptized' it in the seventh century by adding 'Christe eleison'.

Christ, the Rising Sun

Early Christians called Christ their 'sun' referring to his resurrection, and thought of the Church as the moon shining with Christ's reflected light. Christ rose from the dead on the day sacred to Helios, the day of the sun, and early on, the Christian feasts of Sunday and Easter were established. In the late first century, Ignatius of Antioch spoke of Christians who die for their faith as sharing in the sunset and sunrise of Christ. Writing to Christians in Rome about his own approaching death, he reasoned: 'It is a fair thing to sink like the sun from this world, so that I may have my sunrise with God' (Kleist 1946, p.81).

Ancient peoples thought that the sun descended into the underworld at night, so early Christians described Christ in similar terms. Like the sun setting in the evening, Christ descended into the underworld; like the sun crossing the dark region beneath the earth, Christ visited the just in the land of the dead; and like the sun rising next morning with renewed splendour, Christ rose again in glory. Good Friday was seen as the day of Christ's sunset, and Easter day that of his sunrise. Since the rising sun was a symbol of divinity, people in most ancient cultures, including those of Greece and Rome, turned to the east to pray, the place where the sun rises, from which life, power and happiness therefore originate. Christians also turned to the east to pray and built their churches and graves facing east. Paradise was situated in the east (*Genesis* 2:8), and Christ ascended to the east of Jerusalem. In the book of *Revelation*, the angels at the end of time come from the east (*Revelation* 7:2), and Christ was expected to follow them. So when Christians prayed facing east, they were turning towards the glorified Christ, ready to greet his return. In a fifth century sermon, Pope Leo the Great deplored the fact that when Roman Christians climbed the steps leading up to St. Peter's, they turned around to bow before the rising sun. But a ceiling mosaic in a third century Christian tomb beneath St. Peter's portrays Christ as the sun god driving the sun chariot, with his hands on his horses' reins and light spreading out before him (Jungmann 1960, pp.23–24, 135–137).

Sunday

In the first century BC it became a universal custom to name the seven days of the week after the seven planets, a tradition coming perhaps from Persian and Egyptian astrology. Christ rose on the day of the sun, and Ignatius of Antioch in the late first century used the Greek word for sunrise when he described Christians as 'those who no longer adhere to the sabbath, but live according to the day of the Lord on which our life rose' (Letter to the Magnesians). In Rome, Sunday was a working day following Saturn's day of rest, and Christian worship on the day of the sun was so unusual that some pagans thought Christians were sun-worshippers. In the mid-second century Tertullian wrote: 'Others…mistake the sun for the Christian God because they have heard that in praying we turn towards the rising sun, and because on the day of the sun we give ourselves over to joy—though this last has nothing to do with any religious honour paid to the sun'. As sun worship spread in the late Roman empire, however, Romans began to count Sunday, not Saturday, as the first day of the week (Rahner (i) 1963, pp.104–107).

The daily setting of the sun symbolised death to ancient Greeks. In the far west, where the sun sinks into the sea, they imagined the 'gates of Hades' which the sun god entered each evening, travelling eastwards by a hidden road, to rise next morning. Applying this to Christ, St. Augustine wrote: 'The passion of Christ is the setting of Christ'. In his gospel, Matthew noted that 'there was darkness over the earth' at Christ's death (*Matthew* 27:45), and Luke commented that 'the sun was darkened' (*Luke* 23:45). St. Jerome explained the darkening of the sun as a sign of its shame at the setting of Christ, the true sun, and Carolingian miniatures of the crucifixion show the sun growing red with shame and hiding its head. Pagans believed that the kingdom of demons, death and darkness lay in the west, so on Easter eve, candidates for baptism faced west to denounce Satan. Cyril of Jerusalem reminded his newly baptised Christians: 'First you went into the antechamber of the baptistry and there, facing the sunset,…you stretched forth your hand, and with this gesture you renounced Satan,…for the sunset is the region of visible darkness, while Satan is darkness itself, and has the empire over darkness. To express this by means of a symbol, you look towards the sunset, and in this way you renounce this dark and sinister ruler' (Rahner (i) 1963, pp.113–117, 124).

Easter Night

There are hints of Christ's redemptive journey through Hades in the letters of saints Peter (1 *Peter* 3:19; 4:6) and Paul (*Ephesians* 4:9). In the second century, Melito of Sardis develops this theme into a wonderful sunscape as he describes Christ driving his chariot into the sea, where the moon and the stars bathe in the baptistry of the sun: 'When, drawn by his fiery steeds, the sun has completed his daily course, …then, almost lost from view, he descends into the ocean… Bathing himself in the mysterious depths, he shouts mightily for joy, for water is his nourishment. He remains one and the same, yet he comes forth strengthened out of the depths, a new sun, and shines his light upon us, having been cleansed in the water. And now he has made the darkness of night to flee away and brought us the shining day. There follow him in due course the dancing ranks of the stars, and by reason of him, the moon puts forth her power. They bathe in the baptistry of the sun, like those who are obedient under instruction, and it is only because the moon and stars follow the course of the sun that they shine with a truly pure light' (Rahner (i) 1963, p.116).

In the Easter vigil, the Easter candle is the symbol of Christ, the unconquered sun. It is dipped into water from which the children of light will rise. The emperor Constantine, who was a sun-worshipper before he became a Christian loved the symbol of light at the Easter vigil. Eusebius records that 'Constantine turned night into day during these nocturnal solemnities by setting up enormous pillars of wax which burned all through the night before Easter. They were like flaming torches which made this nocturnal vigil brighter than the shining day'. In an early baptismal hymn among the 'Odes of Solomon', a Christian describes how baptism has changed him:

> As the sun is a joy to those who seek the daylight,
> So is my joy in the Lord, for he is my sun.
> His rays have raised me up,
> His light has wiped all darkness from my face.
> Through him have I received eyes, and now I behold the day.
> I have left the ways of error: to him have I gone
>
> (Rahner (i) 1963 p.126).

Christmas

The Christian feast of Christmas did not develop until the late third century; it was celebrated on 25th December because this was the pagan feast of the birthday of the unconquered sun. The feast came from the East, where sun cults originated, and celebrated the point in the year at which the sun, after losing its power with diminishing daylight, became newborn and grew strong again. Emperor Aurelian introduced the feast to Rome in 274 AD in order to unify religion in his empire. He built a huge temple to the sun, appointed a college of priests and made 25th December a national holiday (Jungmann 1960, pp.23–24, 135–137). The Greeks and Romans thought of birthdays as a kind of sunrise, and the Christian Clement of Alexandria wrote that 'sunrise is the symbol of a birthday'. As the birthday of Christ, the feast of Christmas was designed to combat and consecrate the sun cults of Greece and Rome. While the pagans noisily celebrated the birthday of the unconquered sun, St. Augustine (fifth century) preached about Christ the newborn sun: 'Let us rejoice, my brothers, however, much the pagans may shout, for it is not the visible sun that makes this day holy, but its invisible maker'. Next Christmas he preached: 'Yes, my brothers, we will keep this day holy, but not like the unbelievers because of the sun, but because of him who is the sun's creator (Rahner (i) 1963, pp.132, 150–151).

Christmas was a Roman feast; its Greek equivalent was the Epiphany, a late third century birthday feast whose name means 'illumination'. In the ancient East, the winter solstice was a feast of the Egyptian sun god Osiris. Since leap years were not accurately calculated, the feast day gradually shifted to 6th January of the Julian calendar. A letter of St. Epiphanius describes a winter solstice feast celebrated on 6th January in towns of Egypt and Arabia in honour of the birth of Aion, daughter of the virgin Kore. That night, temple processions were held, with cries of 'The virgin has brought forth: the light is increasing!' St. John Chrysostom (fourth century) calls Epiphany the birthday of Christ, and it became an Eastern baptism feast in which the Church brought forth new children from the womb of the baptismal pool (Nocent 1977, p.263).

Mary, the Moon

The cry 'The virgin has brought forth!' would not sound too unusual in ancient cultures in which the title virgin meant something like 'one-in-herself', or 'belonging to herself alone'. To be a virgin meant to be unmarried, not related to someone as wife or counterpart. Virgin birth was characteristic of the moon goddess, the great mother who watched over humanity from the sky. Many of the moon goddesses of the ancient world reigned together with their son, who was often a dying and resurrecting god. Since his resurrection would express the new life of spring after winter, it is understandable that early Christian converts should accept Christian teachings of a virgin mother of God and her dying, resurrecting son. Until the time of the crusades, the moon mother and her dying sun were revered in Eastern Asia and Syria (Harding 1971, pp.100–105).

Luna (Greek: Selene) was the Roman moon goddess, and the sister of Apollo, as Selene was the sister of Helios. She began her journey across the sky in the evening, as her brother finished his. Selene was often represented enthroned on the moon, as was Mary in medieval art. In France, peasants still call the moon 'nôtre dame' and in Portugal 'the mother of God'. The Church fathers called Mary 'perfect moon', 'star of the sea' and 'ruler of the ocean'. Pope Innocent III described how sinners could look to the reflected light of Mary: 'Towards the moon it is he should look, who is buried in the shadow of sin and iniquity. Having lost divine grace, the day disappears, there is no more sun for him; but the moon is still in the horizon. Let him address himself to Mary; under her influence thousands every day find their way to God' (Harding 1971, p.100).

The book of *Revelation*, written at the end of the first century AD, records how John the evangelist in exile in the Roman penal colony of Patmos and his disciples interpreted the signs of their times. One of the visions John records is that of the young Church as a pregnant mother: 'Now a great sign appeared in heaven: a woman, adorned with the sun, standing on the moon, and with the twelve stars on her head for a crown. She was pregnant and in labour, crying aloud in the pangs of childbirth' (*Revelation* 12: 1–2). The Church fathers referred the woman standing on the moon and clothed with the sun to both Mary and the Church. On Christmas night a virgin mother gave birth to the Lord, and on

Easter night, new Christians were born from the womb of the baptismal water of the Church. St. Augustine explains that Mary prefigures the childbearing Church: both are 'the woman that is clothed with the sun, with Christ, the Sun of Righteousness.'

The Church as the Moon

The Greeks and Romans thought of the sun and moon as bridal brother and sister carrying out an eternal dance in the heavens, as the moon received light from the sun and passed it on to the other stars. Plutarch explained poetically: 'The moon, in her love for him, circles continually around the sun, and it is by her union with him that she receives the power to give birth'. St. Ambrose applied this to the Church, and told his people to observe the moon 'not only with the fleshly eye, but with the living and penetrating power of the spirit, for the creator has granted this bridal sister-star of the sun the power of showing forth the mystery of Christ'(Rahner (i) 1963, pp.159, 169). The ancient Greeks thought of the moon as mother of the waters, and the principle of all birth. With the sun's heat, she created dew, which enabled grass and animals to grow, and women to bear children. Writing in the late third century, Methodius of Philippi applied this to Mary and the Church: as the virgin Mary gave birth to Christ, receiving into herself the rays of the Christmas sun, so the Church, like a true mother, gives life to the faithful in the waters of baptism. Mary was all pure; one reason why the Church condemned Galileo was that he examined the moon through his telescope and dared to assert that its surface was pocked with craters. This contradicted the traditional image of the moon as a flawless symbol of the virgin mother.

Ancient peoples observed the moon as it waned, disappeared and grew radiant once more, and for both pagans and Christians it was a holy thing to suffer in sympathy with the waning moon. St. Ambrose wrote: 'It is for you that the moon suffers, as she waits with ever-growing longing for your redemption'. Early Christians felt that at the crucifixion, not only was the sun darkened but the moon sorrowfully hid her face, for the prophet Isaiah had declared 'the moon shall be confounded and the sun ashamed' (Isaiah 24:23). Easter takes place on the Sunday following the first full moon after the spring equinox, and Augustine explained how the moon of the Church died with the crucified sun and vanished into the sunset of the crucified, dark with the sinfulness of her people and red with the blood of her martyrs, as she moved towards the full moon of the resurrection at Easter (Rahner (i) 1963, pp.169–171).

Sacred Fire

In some cultures the moon goddess was thought of as being the fire or light of the moon. The goddess Diana was also called Vesta (Latin for torch or candle), and a perpetual fire was kept burning in her temple in Rome. Her chief festival, the feast of torches or candles, was celebrated on 15th August, when her groves shone with torches. This feast is now celebrated by the Church as a festival of Mary, taken into heaven to reign there as queen. In some tribes, women were set apart as priestesses of the moon, with the responsibility of fostering her fertilizing power. They did this by caring for the water supply and tending a sacred fire, which might not be extinguished since it represented the fertilizing light or power of the moon. In Rome, the vestal virgins guarded Vesta's sacred fire and performed ceremonies to regulate the water supply by throwing manikins, which would originally have been human offerings, into the river Tiber.

In Celtic countries the moon mother was worshipped under a different form, that of the goddess Bridgit, whose name means valour, or might. She was a triune moon goddess who represented the moon in its three phases, and a new fire was kindled in her honour on 1st February. In Christianity she became St. Bridget, whose feast was also held on 1st February, and whose nuns were said to tend a sacred fire through several centuries. Candles are now blessed on the feast of Candlemas, 2nd February, in honour of Mary bringing her child to the temple. In the North of England, Candlemas was called 'the wives' feast day' and was regarded as a fertility festival (Harding 1971, pp.128–131).

The ancient Israelites used both fire and light in their worship. In the book of *Numbers*, Moses ordered the construction of a lampstand with seven lamps to burn in their holy place (*Numbers* 8:2), and animals were burnt on the altar as offerings in large quantities. To the Israelites, fire revealed the burning holiness of God, which purifies without destroying creation. They expressed this in the story of how Moses first experienced God in a burning bush: 'Moses was looking after the flock of Jethro, his father-in-law…and came to Horeb, the mountain of God. There the angel of the Lord appeared to him in the shape of a flame of fire coming from the middle of a bush. Moses looked; there was a bush blazing but it was not being burned up. "I must go and look at this strange sight," Moses said, "and see why the bush is not burned." Now the Lord saw him go forward to look, and God called to him from the middle of the bush. "Moses, Moses!" he said. "Here I am," he answered. "Come no nearer," he said. "Take off your shoes, for the place on which you stand is holy ground…" At this, Moses covered his face, afraid to look at God' (*Exodus* 3:1–6).

Since light was difficult to obtain and carry round, ancient peoples often kept a fire burning day and night in a public building. Ancient Egyptians had a fire in every temple, and Persians, Greeks and Romans kept a fire in their towns and villages. Since fire also symbolises divinity, a lamp is kept alight continually in Catholic churches, and eternal lamps are found in synagogues. Primitive communities thought such elements as fire and water were holy because they were lifegiving, and the communal fire became a sacred place, with temple, tribunal and town hall grouped around it, and business transacted beside it. If the fire in the Roman temple of Vesta was accidentally extinguished, all public and private business had to stop, for the connection between heaven and earth was felt to have been severed. Greek and Roman armies took live coals from the sacred hearth with them on their expeditions; the twelve Attic tribes brought their firebrands to the altar of Athene Polias in Athens as a sign of their union, and inhabitants of the Greek islands fetched their new fire each year from Delos. In the same way, Greek Orthodox pilgrims flock to Jerusalem each Easter to be present as the new fire is kindled, and take home a candle lit from the sacred flame (Reclus 1910–11, p.400).

The Hearth of Vesta

According to Ovid, the temple of Vesta was originally thatched, and had walls of woven osiers; archaeologists believe that its circular shape dates back to the huts of primitive Rome. The fire burning continually on its altar originated in early times when fire was precious and carefully tended, perhaps by daughters of the tribal leader, in whose house it would be kept for greater safety. The archaic simplicity of the vestal virgins' duties and their homely character imply that their ritual grew out of the domestic routine of early times. They had to fetch water on their heads from a distant fountain, and cook special salt cakes from the first ears of ripe grain, pounding them in a mortar. They performed all their tasks with simple clay tools. On 1st March they decorated the temple with bay or laurel, and rekindled the sacred fire by rubbing wood against a plaque cut from a fruit tree. The religious ceremonies in which they took part were the oldest Italian agricultural festivals of harvest, vintage and Lupercalia (Masson 1965, pp.57–60).

Because their tasks were considered to be holy, the vestal virgins became privileged religious women. Their house in the Roman forum was built around a long, elegant courtyard surrounded by marble colonnades, with three pools in the centre. The second century house consisted of great walled enclosures surrounding peaceful cloisters, resembling the austere convents for high-ranking ladies in Christian Rome. They lived in style, with spacious rooms on the ground floor of their house, and two or even three upper storeys. There were only six priestesses, two of whom would be quite young, since they were recruited between the ages of six and ten. Their long, detailed ritual took ten years to learn. Their hair was cut off when they entered the sisterhood, as was that of nuns until recently; when it grew again, it was dressed in archaic style. They wore long white robes clasped with a brooch, their only ornament. Their lives were austere, but highly privileged. If one of them allowed the sacred fire to go out, she was scourged for causing a national calamity, and if she broke her vow of 30 years' virginity she could be buried alive; but vestals could resign and marry if they wished. Few did so, for the state gave them a large dowry to spend as they wished, and socially they took precedence over everyone except the empress: only she and they were allowed to drive through Rome in carriages, and consuls made way for them in the streets. The vestal virgins were so highly esteemed that their order survived until 394 AD, after the emperors had become Christian (Masson 1965, pp.58–60). The vestal virgins lived well into the time of the virgin martyrs. According to the *Acts* of St. Agnes, the Roman governor urged her to become a vestal virgin in an attempt to save her life.

The Easter Fire

The Christian Easter vigil, which developed in the fourth century, opens with the blessing of a sacred fire. It is prepared outside the church, and the people gather in the darkness for the priest to light and bless the new fire. In the flickering flames he next turns to the Easter candle which he dedicates to Christ and then lights from the fire. He brings it into the dark church as the deacon sings 'Christ our light!' The people respond with 'Thanks be to God!' as they light their tapers from the Easter candle, until the church glows with candlelight. Thus fire and light are drawn into the worship of the Church on the first Sunday after the first full moon of springtime. Perhaps the simplest praise of these great lights is found in the 'canticle of the sun' which Francis of Assisi composed in the early thirteenth century, and sang to a tune he made up:

> All praise be yours, my Lord, through all that you have made,
> And first my Lord Brother Sun,
> Who brings the day; and light you have given us through him.
> How beautiful he is, how radiant in all his splendour!
> Of you, Most High, he bears the likeness.
> All praise be yours, my Lord, through Sister Moon and Stars;
> In the heavens you have made them, bright
> And precious and fair...
> All praise be yours, my Lord, through Brother Fire,
> Through whom you brighten up the night.
> How beautiful he is, how glad! Full of power and strength...
> Praise and bless my Lord, and give him thanks,
> And serve him with great humility
> (Armstrong and Brady 1982, pp.38–39).

Celtic Prayers of Fire and Light

In the 19th century, Alexander Carmichael spent 60 years recording songs in the Outer Hebrides, and found the deeply religious islanders still chanting songs to bless fire, sun and moon. At daybreak, housewives kindled the fire by lifting the peat which smothered it the previous night. One kindling song goes:

> I will kindle my fire this morning
> In the presence of the holy angels in heaven...
> Without malice, without jealousy, without envy,
> Without fear, without terror of anyone under the sun,
> But the Holy Son of God to shield me... (De Waal 1988, p.74).

An Islander recalled: 'In my father's time there was not a man in Barra but would take off his head covering to the white sun of the day, nor a woman in Barra but would incline her body to the white moon of the night'. They welcomed the sun with such beautiful chants as this one:

> The eye of the great God,
> The eye of the God of glory,
> The eye of the King of hosts,
> The eye of the King of the living,
> Pouring upon us at each time and season...
> Glory to thee, thou sun,
> Face of the God of life' (De Waal 1988, p.221).

For these seafarers, the moon lit and guided their coracles as they fished among reefs and rocks. 'Queen-maiden' moon is addressed in this song:

> She of my love is the new moon,
> The King of all creatures blessing her;
> ... Holy be each thing which she illumines;
> Kindly be each deed which she reveals...
> May the virgin of my love
> Be coming through dense dark clouds
> To me and to each one
> Who is in tribulation.
> May the King of grace
> Be my helping hand... (De Waal 1988, p.226).

Sun, moon and fire were experienced as wonders of God by people living so close to creation. These islanders sang to God during sowing and reaping, when milking and churning, while smothering the fire and kindling it again. They were deeply in touch with the lifegiving power of natural symbols.

CHAPTER 7

Symbols of Jesus and Mary in Art

From the time of the prehistoric cave-painters to the Renaissance, artists attached greater importance to the subject matter of their paintings than to their form and style. Today we are perhaps less familiar than ever before with the Christian and classical themes that western artists chose as the subjects of their paintings, so it can be difficult for us to see paintings as their artists wished them to be seen. Christian artists constantly used symbols in their art, from the catacomb painters for whom a dove stood for the Holy Spirit and a fish for Christ to the seventeenth century Dutch and Flemish still-life painters who conveyed the vanity of human life by a skull and hour-glass, or recalled holy communion with a loaf of bread, a jug and a bunch of grapes.

Male and Female

In many ancient cultures, the language of symbol developed as a system of dualities or opposites. Many natural objects can be seen to have opposite phases or aspects; day and night, summer and winter, man and woman, earth and sky. Night is unlike day; they are counterbalanced forces of opposite poles, and opposites form a whole. This is the basis of the ancient Chinese philosophy of yin and yang. Many cultures came to the same conclusions about what is male and what is female. Early man and woman were quite conscious of their bodies, since they did not cover themselves with layers of clothing. Everyone knew that a woman was pregnant for nine months, and they related the moon to the female body. One can imagine early man saying to early woman: 'The moon is more like you. It changes its shape like you do. I don't change my shape'. Again, the moon has a twenty-eight day cycle like the woman's menstrual cycle. Man, on the other hand, is more like the sun: he doesn't change his shape. The sun gives light, and the moon receives it; the male gives his seed, and the female receives it. Early peoples came to think of the female as representing the moon, night, darkness and black, while the male represented the sun, day, light and white.

The female also represents earth, for seeds are sown in the earth and nurtured in a hidden way, as a mother nurtures her child in her womb, while the male is not so closely connected with the earth. Today our relationship with the earth is one of expediency, but an American Indian refused to work at strip-mining saying, 'If I rape mother earth now, she will not receive me back into her bosom when I die'. The mother who is giver of all, mother of gods, people and animals, occurs in many primitive mythologies. She may be called moon mother or earth mother ('mother nature'), and she was often seen as both, since each represents the same lifegiving power. Chaldeans, Greeks and Scandinavians described their mother goddesses as both lunar and earth deities (Harding 1971, pp.95–96).

Language tells us how people viewed things as male or female. Sun, for example, is masculine in most languages (Latin: *sol*) and moon feminine (Latin: *luna*). Dawn is usually female, and Mary is symbolised by Venus, the morning star; when the scriptures speak of Christ the morning star, they refer to the rising sun. Dusk is symbolically represented as a man chased by a woman, night, who is waiting to fling over him her great mantle of darkness. Dawn and dusk were considered to be time outside time, the time of lovemaking, and the time of making love to God in prayer. Dawn and dusk have always been the Church's times for prayer.

Mary, Queen of Heaven and Earth

In Christian art, Mary took over the function of Luna and Selene as Queen of the Heavens. Mary appears wearing a dark blue mantle for she is clothed with the night sky, often with a star on her head and another on her shoulder; sometimes her mantle is filled with gold stars. She may stand on the moon, with twelve stars round her head for a crown, an image taken from the book of *Revelation* (12:1). Sometimes her mantle is the silver grey of dawn and dusk, or black like the night sky, although in eastern art it may be brown, the colour of earth. Mary is portrayed as Queen of the Heavens in other forms: sometimes she is shown being assumed or drawn into heaven at her death. She rises into the sky, resting on a cloud and surrounded by angels. The coronation of Mary as Queen of Heaven was another subject of medieval art: Christ, her consort, places a crown on her head, or his Father may do so. In later paintings, Mary stands on a crescent moon, as did the goddesses Luna and Selene.

The Romans considered Luna and Diana (goddess of the earth) to be aspects of the same deity, and in the same way, Mary was considered as Queen of Heaven and also Queen of Earth. A mother figure (*telluris mater*: earth mother) was a central object of worship in many religions, and Mary's rich iconography seems to have grown over the centuries out of the need of the Christian Church for a mother figure. The image of the mother and child had long existed in pagan religions: the Egyptian goddess Isis was portrayed holding her son Horus on her lap, and this image survived well into Christian times in some Mediterranean countries. Sometimes Isis was portrayed suckling her son, and the most ancient image of Mary and her son is *virgo lactans*: Mary suckling the infant

Christ. The unicorn was associated with the worship of a virgin mother goddess, and became linked with the virginity of Mary and the birth of Christ. The horn of this mythical beast had the power to purify whatever it touched, and it could be captured only by a virgin; it was seen to represent Christ. There are sculptures of the unicorn in romanesque and gothic churches, and it is the subject of fifteenth and sixteenth century tapestries in northern Europe. The unicorn is often portrayed in an enclosed garden (another symbol of Mary), beside a woman holding a mirror. The mirror was another emblem of the mother goddess, and the flawless mirror became a symbol of Mary's virginity (Hall, pp.327–328).

Mary, the Earth Mother

The ancient Israelites were often attracted by the worship of Astarte, the fertility goddess of their Canaanite neighbours; her image was the 'asherah', a snake coiled round a tree. The Israelite king Hezekiah was commended for destroying the asherah (2 *Kings* 18:4), although the serpent on a pole erected by Moses in the desert was probably an asherah. In Roman mythology Ceres was the goddess of agriculture, and was worshipped as the earth mother and the source of fertility; her Greek name was Demeter. As the summer goddess she was depicted wearing a crown of corn or carrying a horn of plenty overflowing with fruit. Her daughter Proserpine (Greek: Persephone) was the goddess of spring-time, and the Romans also honoured Flora, goddess of flowers in spring. Medieval Christians honoured Mary as their May Queen, strewing her way with flowers as they processed through the streets in her honour. Mary took on aspects of both Demeter and Persephone. In some paintings she wears flowered garments, or is set in a garden of flowers; in others, such as those of Crivelli, she is surrounded by opulent fruit, or holds fruit in one hand and the infant Jesus with the other. Mary is seen as an enclosed garden cared for by God, an image taken from *The Song of Songs*, a collection of Old Testament love poems probably dated from the fifth century BC, in which the bridegroom says of his bride:

> She is a garden enclosed,
> my sister, my promised bride;
> a garden enclosed, a sealed fountain...
> I come into my garden,
> my sister, my promised bride (*Song of Songs* 4:12; 5:1).

In medieval paintings, Mary is often portrayed in a rose garden, the rose being an ancient symbol of love. In Mary's bower, red roses for love and white ones for purity are entwined. Sometimes lilies are growing there too, another ancient symbol of purity. Mary's association with roses continues into the rosary, and the imagery of later visionaries such as Bernadette of Lourdes.

In some paintings, Mary or her son holds an apple, a reference to Eden, and Christ's saving work. Grapes symbolise the blood of Jesus and the wine at Mass.

The pomegranate was the ancient attribute of Persephone, who each spring renewed the earth with life; it became associated with the resurrection and immortality. The child Christ often holds a bird, symbolising the flight of the soul at death; frequently he clutches a goldfinch, a favourite Italian cage bird and children's pet. The red splash on a goldfinch's head is said to be a drop of Christ's blood shed on Calvary. In northern Europe in the seventeenth century, Catholic traditions were pruned away under Protestant influence, but this scheme of symbolism was kept by artists in still life paintings, in which their choice and arrangement of objects formed a statement of Christian belief (Hall, p.330).

Sometimes Mary is portrayed gathering the faithful beneath her dark blue mantle, protecting her children in the darkness. Her power to affect the exterior world resides in her outer garment. The prophet Elijah bequeathed his mantle to his disciple Elisha, and when Elisha hurled it at the Jordan, the river parted for him to walk across (2 Kings 2:7–15). The soldiers divided Christ's mantle into four parts, symbolically spreading his power to the four corners of the globe (John 19:23). Sir Walter Raleigh took off his cloak for Queen Elizabeth I to walk over, thus divesting himself of his power. Religious wear mantles symbolising spiritual power, and magicians appear swirling their black cloaks around to display their magic power; Superman's power resides in his cloak. We cannot give away our inner garment, for it symbolises inner psychic and spiritual power. Christ's inner garment could not be rent, for he remained whole (John 19:23–24), but the high priest rent his garments, showing the lie in his statement that Jesus deserved to die: he had condemned a just man falsely, and caused a rift in his own psyche (Mark 14:63). Mary's inner garment is usually gold or rose-coloured, the colour of love, of blood and of the Holy Spirit (Moots 1984).

The Pregnancy of Mary

The first story in the life of Christ which medieval painters loved to illustrate was the annunciation or invitation from God to Mary, in which the angel Gabriel asked her if she would conceive the Son of God (Luke 1:26–38). Painters depicted the action on two levels: at the top of the painting God the Father sends a dove down a sunbeam to hover over Mary's head, as the life-bringing Spirit. Meanwhile, Gabriel appears from the left of the painting to deliver his message to Mary. In early paintings, Mary receives the angel in all her dignity as queen of the earth, seated on a throne richly draped with crimson hangings. The annunciation takes place at the moment between the Old and New Testaments, and in paintings such as those of Piero della Francesca, arches reverberate backwards and forwards in space and time to emphasise the eternal implications of Mary's answer to the angel. In early annunciation paintings there is a clear dividing line between Mary, who represents time, and Gabriel, who represents eternity; the angel stretches out his hand into Mary's space to indicate that eternity is breaking into time. Since Mary is an enclosed garden cared for by God, she sometimes wears flowered garments; she is the new garden of Eden which God is beginning to cultivate. Often a lily appears in the painting: Gabriel may hold it, and then plant it in a vase beside Mary. The lily represents Christ contained in the vessel of Mary's womb. In some paintings the angel's greeting to Mary is written in gold letters through the air between them, and Mary's answer is painted in mirror writing, as she sends her reply back to God (Moots 1984).

After Mary agreed to become the mother of God, St. Luke tells us that she went to visit her cousin Elizabeth in the Judaean hills, for Elizabeth was soon to give birth to John the Baptist (*Luke* 1:39–58). Artists frequently painted this scene, attracted by the poignancy of the encounter between the two pregnant women. In some romanesque sculptures of the visitation, one sees a cross-section of the wombs of Mary and Elizabeth. Jesus is seated in Mary's womb; in Elizabeth's, John the Baptist kneels in reverence to his Lord. In later art the encounter is expressed with more sophistication as a meeting of eyes: Mary's eye meets Elizabeth's, almost forming a single Picassoesque face. The word 'pupil' of the eye comes from the same root as 'pupa' (child), for the pupil represents the child in the womb of the white of the eye. Ancient Egyptians described the 'Divine Eye' as the sun in the mouth, the word in the mouth, or the creative word. We think of the eye as the window of the soul, for our eyes speak our thoughts. Jung considered the eye to be the maternal bosom, and the pupil to be the child returning to his mother's bosom (Cirlot 1962, pp.99–101). So Mary's eye meets her cousin's, as their two children meet to begin their saving work.

The Birth of Jesus

After the visitation, Mary returned home and gave birth to her child in Bethlehem (*Luke* 2:1–6). The nativity of Jesus is symbolised by the star, a tiny light breaking into the darkness. The star in nativity paintings shines from above, from the direction of God the Father. In American Indian mythology, messages from the gods came from the north star through a hole in the sky onto the tip of the sacred mountain at the north pole, and so to us. In many mythologies, north symbolises the Father, east the Son, south the Spirit and west death. Like the sun, we rise in the morning of life (east) and set in death in the evening of life (west). The legend of Father Christmas combines the Norse myth of Odin's chariot racing across the darkened skies as he showered presents on the children of northern lands with the story of the fourth century bishop Nicholas of Myra who visited poor families with gifts of gold (Green 1983, p.93). Father Christmas embodies symbolic truths; he comes from the north, and is bearded like a father. He brings gifts, and the most precious gift of the Father, his son Jesus. He lives at the top of the mountain, as gods do, and breaks through into our world at midnight. He comes down the chimney and out through the fireplace, a symbol of birth from the womb. The Yule log blazing in the hearth is another symbol of birth taking place in the womb. The candles on our Christmas trees refer to Christ, the star breaking into our darkness. In the American southwest the Christmas luminarios, or candles placed in sand inside small bags, are traditionally explained as lights to guide the Christ child on his way.

The nativity took place in a cave in the mountain; God became man in a cave which is the mouth, or womb, of the mountain. In early cultures, the back room of the house was a cave, and the front room was a flimsy shelter added at the mouth of the cave. Some American Indian pueblos show this design: the front room was a small shelter to protect from the sun, while the cave, the back room, provided protection, warmth in winter and coolness in summer. In the Old Testament, significant encounters took place in caves, for the cave is the interior of the mountain, a sacred, mysterious inner space. David encountered King Saul in a cave (1 *Kings* 19:9–18), and the prophet Elijah experienced God at the entrance to a cave (1 *Kings* 19:9–18). In Nazareth, the place venerated as the site of the annunciation is a cave; Jesus was born in a cave and buried in a cave. In early paintings, John the Baptist is portrayed at the mouth of a cave: the mouth of the cave of Elizabeth's womb, and the cave of his prison, the scene of his heavenly birth. The cave can be a symbol of the human person: the mountain becomes the body, and the cave is its mouth. The inner space of the mountain is holy: in an ancient Hawaian burial rite, the dead body is put into a boat and steered into a sea cave, till it slips down into the interior of the mountain (Moots 1984).

The ox and ass are normally portrayed worshipping the infant Jesus in the crib; in romanesque art they are often at the centre of the scene, their heads leaning over the manger, while Mary and Joseph look on from a distance. The gospels do not mention the animals; Luke merely tells us that Mary laid her child in a manger, but medieval artists took their cue from a phrase of Isaiah: 'The ox knows its owner and the ass its master's crib' (*Isaiah* 1:3). The baby is tightly wrapped in swaddling clothes, and may be lying on what resembles an altar in romanesque sculpture, to foreshadow Christ offered on the altar at Mass. The sculptor reminds us that this infant will be similarly laid out in the tomb; the manger may even resemble a tomb. In later medieval art, Mary looks down lovingly at her babe, as she gradually moves to the centre of the scene. By the twelfth century, the mother and her child are increasingly portrayed on their own. People loved to dwell on the tenderness of their relationship, and as devotion to the mother and child grew, artists came to paint this scene more than any other. In other nativity paintings, angels bring the news of Christ's birth to the shepherds. While the shepherds represent the Jews coming to adore their messiah, the magi represent the gentile world. They bring precious gifts and in later art they are portrayed as coming from the three known continents of Europe, Asia and Africa, one of them being painted as a Moor (Young 1991, pp.45–55).

The Adult Jesus

Paintings of the adult Jesus have varied in emphasis through the centuries. Although portraits survive from well before the time of Jesus, we possess no images of Jesus and his disciples earlier than the third century. This is for several reasons: portraits were painted of important and wealthy people, and Jesus and his followers were not wealthy. Also, devout Jews such as Jesus did not allow pictorial representations of themselves, and although Christianity soon spread beyond the boundaries of Judaism, the young Church was often persecuted, and preferred to represent Christ by signs and symbols. By the fourth century, however, Roman sculptors had begun to depict scenes from the life of Christ on stone coffins, and this presented them with the challenge of how to represent the divine founder of a new religion. Their solution was to revert to familiar models: the youthful god, such as Apollo, the young hero, or the idyllic shepherd. Their choice of the young, radiant god illustrates the optimism and confidence of the fourth century Church, newly recognised by the Emperor Constantine (Weiler 1980, pp.143–145).

The eastern Roman empire, based in Constantinople, did not develop this theme of the youthful god. Byzantine legend claimed that the first images of Jesus, Mary and the apostles were brought to earth by angels, and other traditions claimed that St. Luke was the first person to paint a portrait of Mary. Images were highly venerated until the image controversy which lasted over a hundred years (726–843), when image-breakers destroyed icons to prevent them from being worshipped. Meanwhile, icons remained relatively unchanged in style from the sixth to the eighteenth centuries. They presented Christ as a bearded, mature man, no longer a youthful god, but a teacher, friend and lord. His limbs were concealed by drapery, and the artist focused on the expressiveness of Christ's gaze and the gestures of his hands. He was set in a glimmering background of mosaic, enamel or gold. Western artists took over the use of shimmering gold in order to remove the sacred characters from their earthly setting. The crusades and petty wars of the time led artists to develop a new image of Christ the king, their victorious leader and lord. In early medieval art Jesus is almost always 'Christ the King', wearing a royal crown even on the cross. Often he is portrayed as Lord of Heaven, holding the book of the gospels, his lifegiving law (Weiler 1980, pp.145–149).

John the Baptist

In medieval art, Jesus is frequently contrasted with his cousin John the Baptist. As Jesus's prophet and herald, John said of his cousin 'He must increase, while I must decrease' (*John* 3:30). John's birthday is on 24th June when the sun can be seen to decrease while Jesus's birthday is on 25th December, when the sun starts to increase its light. John is the setting sun in relation to Christ the rising sun: John sets into the waters of death, while Christ rises to begin his life's work.

John fasted while Christ feasted; John wore camel's hair clothing while Christ wore a garment so fine that no one wanted to tear it. One of the symbols often associated with John is the axe, or sword. Early in his preaching John declared that the axe must be laid to the root of the tree; at the end of his life, a sword severed his head. In many legends, a hero has to kill a dragon, but when he cuts off its head the dragon then grows two heads. Each time the hero cuts off another head, more heads grow, so the hero has to retreat and find a wise old woman who will teach him a better strategy. He is usually advised to pierce the dragon's heart, or his heel, or some other secret spot. The hero goes off and does so, and so slays the dragon. John knew that he had to cut the root of the tree of corruption with his axe, for if you cut a tree's branches, you trim it and it only grows stronger. Similarly with dragons, if their heads are cut off, they only grow more. Herod cut off John the Baptist's head but he was afraid he had used the wrong strategy; he wondered if Christ was John come back from the dead (*Mark* 6:16) (Moots 1984).

Before John died, he handed over his work to his cousin Jesus. Their encounter took place in the river Jordan, where John was baptizing. The gospels describe the dramatic scene: as John immersed Jesus in the waters, the voice of the Father was heard like thunder from heaven, and the Spirit hovered overhead in the form of a dove (*Matthew* 3:13–17). Early Christian writers elaborated the imagery: they describe fire bursting forth from the Jordan, the terrified river flooding backwards and angels hurrying to the spot to give the Son of God the white garment of his divine, essential light (Rahner (i) 1963, p.79). In some early paintings of Christ's baptism, the Jordan rises around Christ's waist as the waters worship their Lord, disregarding gravity. By portraying the river rising in spate, artists recalled the story of Joshua leading the Israelites safely through the Jordan, when its 'upper waters stood still and made one heap over a wide space' (*Joshua* 3:7–17). As Moses led his people through the Red Sea and Joshua led them through the Jordan, medieval Christians reflected that they in turn crossed the waters of death through baptism. In the middle ages, converts were baptized by poured water, and this is how artists depicted the baptism of Jesus: John baptizes Jesus in the river, while the Father views the scene from above, a dove hovers over Christ's head and angels hold his garments.

In early mosaics, the river god is pictured fleeing at the sight, for he is now superseded. Other mosaics link Christ's baptism with that of his followers. John the Baptist had said of Jesus: 'See, here is the Lamb of God' (*John* 1:35–36), and apse mosaics in Roman churches portray Christ as a lamb on a small mountain at whose foot the Jordan flows (sometimes labelled 'Jordanes' so there will be no mistake). Four streams of grace, representing the four rivers of paradise, flow down the hillside into the Jordan, and sheep who represent the baptized faithful graze among the streams. Later paintings set the scene in the local countryside and portray Christ wearing richly brocaded garments in the latest style.

In some paintings of the Baptism of Jesus, fish or little people or both are swimming in the Jordan. The fish represent Christians who will be baptized in the wake of Jesus. Sometimes, as at Sant Apollinare Nuovo in Ravenna, apostles sailing in the ship of the Church cast their net to catch fish, who again represent new believers, since Jesus told his friends, 'I will make you fishers of men' (*Matthew* 4:19). The net of the Church is then raised to the heavens, and fish in the sea become stars in the sky, so in medieval paintings stars also represent the faithful. This is an ancient Jewish image, for God promised Abraham: 'I will make your descendants as many as the stars' (*Genesis* 15:6). Developing this theme, St. Paul declared to the early Christians: 'You will shine in the world like bright stars, because you are offering it the word of life' (*Philippians* 2:16). Sometimes, as at the fifth century mausoleum of Galla Placidia in Ravenna, the vault is filled with stars of different shapes, colours and sizes, 'star differing from star in glory' (1 *Corinthians* 15:41), to represent the great variety of holy people. In this mausoleum, the stars gleam like gold and white snowflakes against a deep blue sky, and the mosaic vault of the heavens surrounds a peaceful scene in which the Good Shepherd pastures his faithful flock.

In the life of John the Baptist, dance is significant. At the beginning of his life he danced, or leapt for joy in his mother's womb (*Luke* 1:44) in the same way that King David danced naked before the ark of the covenant, in homage to his Lord (2 *Samuel* 6:14). At the end of John's life, Salome's seductive dance caused his death. When John's head was brought into the banquet at Salome's request, Herod's birthday was being celebrated; today we celebrate not Herod's birthday but John's. In many paintings, John's head is brought in on a golden plate; the plate becomes his halo. In some stories, beheaded saints pick up their heads and walk to the cemetery, singing as they go, to show that they are truly still alive. A primitive Ethiopian painting shows King Herod wielding a sword, about to behead John, since the act originates from him, even though in the painting he is surrounded by guards who could do the deed. In the upper left hand corner of the painting, John's head appears, winged, flying into heaven. In the lower left hand corner, his head appears in glory on a plate. To the lower right is Salome's upper body, her naked breasts hanging seductively, and her bangled arms severed from her shoulders, for she is physically dismembered, while John remains whole (Moots 1984).

The Crucifixion of Jesus

The death of Jesus was preceded not by a death-dealing but by a lifegiving meal, his Last Supper with his friends. It took place in an upper room on Mount Sion in old Jerusalem. People climb mountains in order to communicate with God, for earth touches heaven at the tips of mountains. Jesus went into the hills to pray, and climbed the mountain of Transfiguration and the Mount of Olives to speak with God. In some cultures the temple is built on an artificial mountain, and John the evangelist notes that Jesus died on the hill of Calvary at the time when the passover lambs were being slain on the temple mount, for Jesus is the new passover lamb (*John* 19:14).

The scene in the garden of Calvary echoes that in the garden of Eden. The tree of life grew in Eden, and it grows on Calvary. The tree of the knowledge of good and evil in Eden is replaced by the trees on which the good and evil thieves are crucified. The crucifixion of Jesus represents the absorption of the other side of things into a complete whole: Jesus accepts both the good thief and the bad; he does not condemn the bad thief, but absorbs evil with his prayer, 'Father, forgive them, for they know not what they do' (*Luke* 23:34). Crucifixion paintings highlight the opposites which are present at this powerful moment in cosmic history: the good thief and the bad, the reed (peace) and the spear (war) which the soldiers lift up to Jesus; the sun darkened and the moon ashamed. The four limbs of the cross reach out to the four corners of the globe, and artists such as Fra Angelico portray Jesus pierced through by the soldier's spear, taking the cross into the third dimension and transfixing it in space (Moots 1984).

The Mass

The last supper and the crucifixion are both enacted in the Mass, and medieval artists represented these mighty acts in a variety of ways. Fra Angelico painted a last supper scene in which Jesus is a priest distributing round white communion hosts from a ciborium to his apostles and friends, some of whom stand at the table while others reverently kneel. Other artists portray a priest saying Mass in church before a life-sized crucifix on which Jesus hangs above the altar. Hubert van Eyck's magnificent 'Adoration of the Lamb' depicts Christ as a lamb standing slain upon an altar in heaven, his blood pouring into a chalice, surrounded by throngs of adoring angels and saints. He largely drew his imagery for this from the book of *Revelation*, in which the worshippers in heaven at the end of time are described waving palms of victory and shouting and bowing before Jesus, the slain yet victorious Lamb of God (*Revelation* 14:1–3).

The medieval Church evolved a colour code for the vestments priests wear at Mass which expressed their sensitivity to symbols. The earliest colours used by prehistoric peoples were black, blue or dark, and white, yellow or light. The Church used white vestments for festivals and black vestments for funerals. After these two colours, red was the next to emerge. Traces of painted plaster show that the interiors of ancient Maltese temples were painted red, as are Maltese church interiors to this day. Such peoples as American pueblo Indians use only black, white and red in their pottery. The Church uses red vestments to celebrate her martyrs, representing their blood sown in the earth to give life to the world. Green represents earth, and after Eastertime, when Christ's blood has been sown in the earth of the universe, the Church directs that green vestments be worn until the end of the autumn. Purple is the colour of dawn and dusk, and of expectation. Purple vestments are worn during the four weeks of Advent as the world awaits Christmas, and again during the six weeks of Lent as we await Easter. It also became the colour of sorrow and penance, so purple cloths were draped over paintings and other decorations in churches during Lent. Orange is the colour of flames, ferociousness and cruelty, so there is no orange vestment, but Buddha assumed the orange robe of the condemned criminal, in the same way that Christ on the cross assumed the role of sinful humanity (Moots 1984).

In medieval times there was constant interplay between the ritual and symbol of the Church and the image-world of individuals, for whom worship was well mixed into their lives. In a world without television, videos or even many books, the Church was the educator of most people, whose attitudes to life would be largely formed by sermons and through art. Both Catherine of Siena and Julian of Norwich, two of the greatest religious writers of the four-teenth century, learnt their theology simply from listening to preachers. Indi-viduals responded to Christian symbols and rituals in vivid and personal ways. Catherine of Siena, for example, described the Church as an inn on a bridge in which holy bread and wine are served over the counter. Jesus, she explained, is a bridge for mankind, and not an abstract bridge, but one like the Ponte Vecchio in Florence, cobbled, full of people, with shops, stalls and inns. She pictured God the Father looking down on his world, where people are 'running to the bridge of Christ crucified. They gather together, drunk and on fire with love, and climb the bridge. The bridge of Jesus has walls, and a roof called mercy. Sheltered by this roof, we need not be afraid of the thunderstorms of God's justice. On the bridge is an inn, in which the bread of life is served, and the wine of Christ's blood, so my people won't get exhausted on the road. I ordered my Son's body and blood to be served in this inn because I love you' (Catherine of Siena 1925, p.137).

Catherine pictured the sacrifice of Jesus in other ways. His pierced heart was a cave in which she could live in safety: 'Let your place of refuge be Christ crucified, my only Son', she envisions God the Father as saying; 'Dwell and hide in the cavern of his side. In his open heart you will find love for me and love for your neighbour. Seeing and tasting this love, you will follow his teaching, feeding at the table of the holy cross'. Blood and fire were strong images of life and love for Catherine, who wrote to her closest friend: 'I impose on you nothing but to let yourself drown in the blood and fire pouring from the side of God's Son' (Catherine of Siena 1905, p.157).

The symbolism of the Mass is extraordinarily rich and deep, and its ritual embraces many of the symbols with which this book has so far been concerned. The central action of the Mass is a blessing and sharing of corn, the bread of life, and a cup of wine which signifies the outpoured blood of Jesus and ourselves. Those who share the bread and wine also share the healing work of the good serpent raised high upon the tree of life, and they experience the sunset and sunrise of Christ in the reflected light of their own lives. Taking part in this ritual can effect healing and integration at deep levels of our being; yet this will not be true for everyone, because we relate to symbols differently, and forge our own language of imagery and our own response to life. Each of us has embarked on a unique path to discover our roots and our destiny; on the journey we find that our story is deeply interwoven with that of others, but it is a testimony to the inexhaustible variety of creation and the immense lavishness of God that no lifestory ever duplicates another. The hero-journey of each of us is necessary to complete the unfolding story of the world.

CHAPTER 8

Priest and Shaman
Holy Leaders

The Holy Leader: A Symbol of God

Now that we have examined some major natural symbols and their visual representation in art and iconography, we are better equipped to explore a more complex symbol: that of the holy leader who symbolises, or stands for, God. Spiritual leaders in tribal peoples and in Judaeo-Christianity have much in common, although Christians have so far largely ignored their tribal spiritual roots. It is unfortunate that European colonials and missionaries with their tales of witch-doctors created a wall of prejudice against recognising the spiritual contribution of medicine men and wise women to our world, and it is equally sad that many Christian Churches continue to view tribal religions with ambivalence. However seven years ago Pope John Paul II called a meeting of religious leaders from across the world in Assisi, at which for the first time American Indian tribal chiefs prayed alongside Christians, Jews, Buddhists and Moslems, and such sharing is now more frequent.

Anthropologists studying North Asian peoples found that the Tungus of Manchuria call their spiritual leaders shamans from their word meaning 'to know', because a shaman is one who knows. His task is to tell his people what they need to know, but are unable to learn through human knowledge. The Old Testament prophet Balaam, guiding the Israelites through their enemies in the desert, described his function as one who 'knows the knowledge of the Most High' in the following oracle:

> The oracle of Balaam, son of Beor,
> the oracle of the man with far-seeing eyes,
> the oracle of one who hears the word of God,
> of one who knows the knowledge of the Most High.
> He sees what God makes him see,
> receives the divine answer, and his eyes are opened.
> (*Numbers* 24:5,16).

Inuit (Eskimo) shamans maintain harmony among people, and between their tribe and the natural world. They intercede with the spirit world, treat the sick, and pray for favourable weather and success in hunting. Their leadership includes our roles of doctor, priest, lawyer and judge. A shaman is one who crosses the bridge into the spirit world. He or she can therefore speak God's word to us. Polynesians call them 'god boxes'; the Caribs of British Honduras describe a shaman as a 'telephone exchange between people and God' (Lewis 1971, p.56). This is an updated version of the Old Testament concept of a prophet being a 'mouthpiece' of God. The Book of Exodus describes how God tried to send Moses as his prophet, or mouthpiece, to pharaoh, to demand freedom for the Israelite slaves. Moses objected, fearing he could not speak well enough, so God made a new proposal: Aaron, the brother of Moses, could act as a mouthpiece for his brother. Moses agreed that Aaron should become his 'god box':

> Moses said to God's face, 'I am slow of speech; why should pharaoh listen to me?' God said to Moses, 'See, I make you as a god for pharaoh, and Aaron your brother is to be your prophet. You yourself must tell him all I command you, and Aaron your brother will tell pharaoh to let the sons of Israel leave this land.' (*Exodus* 6:30–7:2).

Moses thus became God's prophet, and Aaron became a prophet of Moses.

Shamans' Tasks

Shamans can be male or female; they are found in North and South America, Southeast India and North Asia; elements of their spiritual leadership are found among archaic peoples everywhere. They appear to have existed since Neolithic times, so they are the earliest known form of spiritual leader. They are still the religious leaders of hunting and gathering tribes, and cattle-raising peoples; the Tungus, who gave us the name 'shaman' raise reindeer (Diószegi 1983 pp.638–639). Shamans use priestly skills of prayer, healing and ritual leadership. They pray, or communicate with the spiritual world, often through going into trance, as Pentecostal Christians today speak 'in the Spirit'. When charismatic Christians pray they may intercede (ask of God) of prophesy (speak a message from God). Shamans do the same; they also interpret the 'signs of the times' to their people to influence their conduct, as do Christian preachers, and reconcile people, as priests do in Confession. Shamans also bless births, marriages and deaths, escorting the dead on their final journey beyond death, much as Christian ministers conduct baptisms, weddings and funerals. These have always been the three major events in our human life.

Because of their spiritual profession, shamans are socially respected, as are priests in other cultures. Since they are busy praying for their people, they cannot hunt and fish, so their community often supports them. The Evenki of northern Siberia set up fish traps in the best spots of the river for their shaman in summer and, in winter, clansmen go hunting for him and present him with furs. The Evenki raise reindeer, and poor families pay their shaman one reindeer a year, while richer families pay him two, three or four reindeer. The ancient Israelites evolved a similar method of supporting the Levites, their tribe of priests, who were Aaron's descendants. When people brought their offerings to God, a Levite burnt their offering and ate what remained: 'One of the sons of Aaron must burn the memorial offering on the altar so that its fragrance will appease God, and after this has been done, Aaron and his sons shall eat the remainder in the form of unleavened loaves... The victim for the sacrifice is to be immolated before God... It is a most holy thing. The priest who offers this sacrifice is to eat it' (*Leviticus* 6:7–9; 18–19). Israelite priests, who owned no land, were thus assured of bread and meat. From this tradition grew our custom of tithing, or offering a tenth of one's produce to the local priest. Tithing was already an ancient custom by the time of the Levitical priesthood for, centuries before, Abraham offered a tenth of all his possessions to the priest Melchisedek (*Genesis* 14:20). When priests are lazy or bad, this system becomes corrupt. Offerings to pay for curing the sick can be expensive too. One North Asian tribe has a saying: 'If the beast becomes ill, the dogs fatten; if man becomes ill, the shamans fatten' (Diószegi 1983, p.639).

Spirit Ladder

Shamans dress in ritual robes to lead ceremonies, as priests wear vestments in many religions. Among North Asian peoples, their services take place at night, in a conical tent-dwelling, or yurt, around a fire. The shaman's chants are partly improvised and partly traditional, and he accompanies himself on a drum. Among some peoples, a tall tree is set into the opening for smoke at the top of the tent, to symbolize the world axis tree which the shaman climbs in spirit so that he can reach the heavens (Diószegi 1983 p.640). Another symbol for the shaman's spiritual ascent is a ladder. Shamans of rival communities can try to make their opponents' spirit ladder collapse while their opponent is conducting a ritual, with harmful effects. At other times, a shaman can send his spirit soaring aloft for sheer joy, in a celebration of communion between those on earth and those departed (Lewis 1971, pp.162, 168).

The concept of a spirit ladder was also familiar to the ancient Israelites. The Old Testament patriarch Jacob dreamed of angels on a ladder to the heavens, as he received God's promise that his family would inherit the land on which he slept: 'Taking one of the stones to be found at that place, Jacob made it his pillow and lay down where he was. He had a dream: a ladder was there, standing on the ground, with its top reaching to heaven; and there were angels of God going up it and coming down. And God was there, standing over him' (*Genesis* 28:11–13). Jesus promised his followers that they would see the same thing: 'I tell you most solemnly, you will see heaven laid open and, above the Son of Man, the angels of God ascending and descending' (*John* 1:51). Later Christian writers developed the theme in another direction; St. Benedict (sixth century) in his *Rule for Monks* urged them to climb the rungs of the ladder of humility, in order to arrive at freedom of spirit, while the English mystic Walter Hilton (fourteenth century) wrote a treatise entitled *The Ladder of Perfection* describing the soul's climb towards God.

Prophetic Inspiration

Shamans lead their people through inspiration: they form a human bridge into the spiritual world. When a new Church arises, it is normally characterized by inspiration. Methodism was moulded by the passionate spirit of John Wesley, as he rode preaching from town to town, and only gradually assumed respectability. Early Quakers placed stress on possession by the Spirit, though silent receptivity is now more typical of Quaker prayer. When believers form an oppressed minority, they tend to retain their inspirational fervour, as can be seen in the black Pentecostal Churches of Africa, America and Britain.

As Churches or nations settle into an organised religion, and especially if it becomes corrupt, prophetic figures arise with a new vision of how their people should seek God. The prophets of ancient Israel carried out this role. Prophets are disliked by those who mistrust such vision; most Israelite prophets were killed by their own people. Western imperialists and mistrustful missionaries branded African medicine men as witch-doctors, while midwives and wise women have often been subjected to witch hunts. American Indian religious leaders have rarely been reverenced by white settlers; similarly, the voodoo cult of Haiti was condemned by the country's ruling white society, although with little foundation; the oppressed black population simply gathered under trees during their rest periods to worship in their own inspirational style, as a respite from their oppression. Christian inspirational leaders have suffered in similar ways, however; in the sixteenth century, Anglicans and Catholics martyred one another for proclaiming their convictions. At other times, society declares its inspirational leaders to be mad: supposedly impartial anthropologists at first classified shamans as insane.

Spiritual Power-Conflicts

In some cultures there is much competition between shamans and aspiring shamans. Power struggles are a common human problem, and spiritual power-sharing can be a problem too. Inspirational leaders rely on inner power, and this can pose the problem of authenticity. The ancient Israelites decided that you could tell a true prophet from a false one if he proclaimed bad news (which would not be in his own interest), and if it came true. Like shamans of today, their ancient Israelite counterparts became involved in trials of spiritual strength. Around 1250 BC, Aaron won such a trial of strength when competing against pharaoh's enchanters, although he could not soften Pharaoh's heart:

> God said to Moses and Aaron, 'If pharaoh says to you, "Produce some marvel," you must say to Aaron, "Take your staff and throw it down in front of Pharaoh, and let it turn into a serpent".'... Aaron threw down

his staff in front of pharaoh and his court, and it turned into a serpent. Then pharaoh in his turn called for the sages and the sorcerers, and with their witchcraft the magicians of Egypt did the same. Each threw his staff down and these turned into serpents. but Aaron's staff swallowed up the staffs of the magicians. Yet pharaoh's heart was stubborn and, as God had foretold, he would not listen to Moses and Aaron (*Exodus* 7:8–13).

Much later (600 BC) the prophet Jeremiah engaged in a spiritual battle with a false prophet named Hananiah. In the temple, the false prophet solemnly proclaimed that God would break the yoke of the oppressive king of Babylon, at which Jeremiah put a yoke round his own neck to declare the opposite. Hananiah then took the wooden yoke off Jeremiah's shoulders and broke it. The story continues, as recorded by one of Jeremiah's disciples: 'After the prophet Hananiah had broken the yoke which he had taken off the neck of the prophet Jeremiah, the word of God was addressed to Jeremiah, "Go to Hananiah and tell him this, 'God says this: You can break wooden yokes? Right, I will make them iron yokes instead! For the Lord of hosts, the God of Israel, says this: An iron yoke is what I now lay on the necks of all these nations'"' (*Jeremiah* 28:1–17). Jeremiah added that Hananiah would die within the year for preaching falsely; Hananiah died. The power of predicting another's death is an uncomfortable quality which some shamans possess. Like Aaron and Jeremiah, shamans in other cultures perform trials of strength. North Asian shamans fight dressed as reindeer or horned cattle, claiming the strength of these powerful beasts.

Sharing Spiritual Power

Another problem with spiritual power is how widely it can be shared. A shaman in a highly structured Siberian Inuit tribe may hold absolute sway over his people, while in more loosely organised African cultures, many priests may serve a single community. There may also be competition to gain superiority. The Yakut of Northeast Siberia believe that the souls of future shamans are reared on a very tall tree in the upper world; the greatest shamans are brought up in nests near the top of the tree, and lesser shamans occupy nests in its lower branches (Diószegi 1983 p.640). Other cultures hold that all can share a shaman's powers. America Plains Indians believe that everyone is called to a ritual quest for vision, or a quest to discover their guardian spirit. They set off on a solitary retreat, with fasting and sacrifice (Brown 1985, p.401).

The ancient Israelites encountered the problem of spiritual power-sharing, as the book of *Numbers* recounts. Their great leader, Moses, complained to God that he could no longer lead his rebellious followers unaided, so God told him to choose seventy wise men to help him. God instructed Moses: 'Bring them to the Tent of Meeting, and let them stand beside you there. I will come down to speak with you; and I will take some of the spirit which is on you and put it on them'. Moses found seventy wise men, but two of them stayed back in the camp.

The spirit came on them too, and they began to prophesy. At this, Moses's eager young adjutant, Joshua, urged his master to silence them. Moses had a broader vision, and retorted: 'Are you jealous on my account? If only the whole people of God were prophets, and God gave his spirit to them all!' (*Numbers* 11:16–30). Later (400 BC) the prophet Joel looked forward to a new age when everyone would be inspired:

> I will pour out my spirit on all mankind.
> Yours sons and daughters shall prophesy,
> your old men shall dream dreams,
> and your young men see visions.
> Even on the slaves, men and women,
> will I pour out my spirit in those days (*Joel* 3:1–2).

On Pentecost morning, when the followers of Jesus had been filled with his Spirit, Peter quoted this prophecy to the amazed crowds, explaining that Joel's words were now being fulfilled (*Acts* 2:16–18).

The Call to Leadership

How does a person become a shaman? Most people in our culture take on jobs through hard work or study, or money, or the job runs in their family. The shaman may depend for his calling on several of these factors, but since his call is to a spiritual task, there is a spiritual element in his call. A Catholic monk or nun would describe their call as a religious vocation; their call must be discerned, or humanly assessed, but it is primarily a spiritual call: a call to enter into a living relationship with more-than-human powers. A call to Christian leadership often begins as a commitment to prayer. The person starts to set aside time in which to communicate with God, in a relationship that will continue to deepen. This demands a withdrawal from human affairs in order to focus on the spiritual world. Among Arctic peoples, someone listening to the call to become a shaman may sit in a withdrawn state on a bed or on the ground, in darkness; he may go away to hide among rocks or climb trees, as he learns to deepen his awareness (Lewis 1971, p.54).

Call Through Affliction

Christian leaders may deepen their call during a serious illness, when withdrawal from their normal human activities is forced upon them. Francis of Assisi (twelfth century) was wounded and taken prisoner for a year in a war between Assisi and Perugia. Soon afterwards, he returned from battle, renounced his inheritance and began a new life of poverty. Ignatius of Loyola (sixteenth century) was wounded by the French at the siege of Pamplona. A cannon ball entered his leg, which was badly set and re-set. During his convalescence he read the life of Christ and stories of the saints. He turned to God and spent a year in prayer near Montserrat, as he restructured his life.

In the first century, St. Paul experienced a shock of a different kind. He was riding to Damascus to persecute Christians there, when he was struck off his horse and blinded. A voice challenged him: 'Saul, Saul, why are you persecuting me?' After three days, his blindness was healed by a Christian named Ananias. Through the prayer of this disciple, Paul was filled with God's Spirit. Ananias 'at once laid his hands on Saul and said, "Brother Saul, I have been sent by the Lord Jesus...so that you may recover your sight and be filled with the Holy Spirit"' (*Acts* 9:1–19).

Like Paul, Francis and Ignatius, a person often becomes a shaman through a traumatic experience or cure. He endures affliction, and transforms it into spiritual energy. The Chukchee in the Arctic compare the shaman's time of preparation to a long and severe illness. In Bali, temple mediums are recruited following an illness which is later seen as a blessing. In Haiti, possession and initiation into the voodoo cult often follows a serious illness or disaster (Lewis 1971, pp.67, 68).

Some shamans prepare for their calling by a struggle with spiritual powers. Jesus struggled with demons for forty days in the desert as he prepared to begin his ministry. St. Mark writes: 'The Spirit drove him out into the wilderness and he remained there for forty days, and was tempted by Satan. He was with the wild beasts, and the angels looked after him' (*Mark* 1:12,13). The Egyptian hermits of the desert continued this pattern: St. Antony (fourth century) lived in the desert for twenty years, struggling with demons. His biographer described how he emerged from the struggle, peaceful and radiant: 'His countenance had a great and wonderful grace...from the joy of his soul he possessed a cheerful countenance, and from his bodily movements could be perceived the condition of his soul (*Athanasius* 1950). Nearer our time, the nineteenth century French priest John Vianney, often known as the Curé d'Ars, struggled with demons while at the same time transforming people through his preaching, his spiritual advice and his healing work in the sacrament of Confession. John Vianney is still regarded as a model by many Catholic priests today.

Inherited Leadership

Leaders may inherit their spiritual power: an old Ethiopian priest sent his son to Addis Ababa for his education, where the Emperor helped him. When his father died, the son fell ill. He did not want to return home to succeed his father as priest of the clan, but finally the Emperor advised him 'You will not get well here, and your education affords you no joy. Return to your father's land and live as your custom bids you'. The son returned home, became a priest and recovered (Knutsson 1967, p.74). American Pueblo Indians are now largely Catholic, but few of them train for priesthood; choosing between two styles of spiritual leadership may be difficult. Around 1980 a Pueblo Indian completed seminary training, but during his ordination ceremony he tripped as he came forward, and broke a leg. He took this as a sign of his calling to lead his people through their own tradition, and decided to do so instead of becoming a Catholic priest. (From a verbatim account given to the author, Albuquerque, New Mexico, 1980.)

Handing on Holiness

In some cultures, shamans hand on their powers without the novice enduring great affliction. In many religions, disciples gather round a great leader, to study and receive his spiritual gifts. North Asian novices observe experienced shamans at work, and do not need to study for their role, since everyone shares the same beliefs (Lewis 1971, p.54). An account of a prophet handing on his power is found in the Old Testament story of Elijah and Elisha (850 BC). The prophet Elijah first called his disciple Elisha by throwing his cloak over him to claim possession of him (1 *Kings* 19:19–21). At the end of the master's life, before being taken up to heaven in a whirlwind, Elijah dropped his cloak, a symbol of his power. His disciple Elisha picked it up, and when he needed to cross the Jordan to rejoin the brotherhood of prophets, he struck the river with his new cloak crying 'Where is the Lord, the God of Elijah?' The account continues: 'He struck the water and it divided to right and left, and Elisha crossed over. The brotherhood of prophets saw him in the distance and said "The spirit of Elijah has come to rest on Elisha"; they went to meet him and bowed to the ground before him' (2 *Kings* 2:2–18).

Holy leadership could be handed on more gently, as we hear in some of the stories of the Jewish rabbis of Eastern Europe. These eighteenth century rabbis sometimes received their vocation as children. Kalman was a five-year old who hid under the rabbi of Berditchev's prayer shawl and looked up into his veiled face. Burning strength entered the boy's heart and took possession of him. Many years later, another rabbi took some of his finest disciples to visit the rabbi of Berditchev, young Kalman being among them. The rabbi of Berditchev looked at him and recognised him. 'That one is mine!', he said (Buber 1947).

Called from Birth

Because spiritual life exists beyond human space and time, a spiritual calling is often described as taking place before birth. Siberian shamans believe that they are chosen and called before birth, and the call can scarcely be resisted. A Southeast Siberian said 'Had I not become a shaman, I would have died' (Diószegi 1983 p.639). Guy Moréchand describes how Hmong shamans are selected in Vietnam and Thailand almost against their will: 'The more he ostensibly refuses this destiny, the more he resists, the more striking will be the signs, the more gripping and dramatic his vocation... Not only have the personal tastes of the individual theoretically no part in this decision to make himself a shaman, but they are also strongly denied. The accent is on the contrary on the acolyte's repugnance: the poor persecuted man who could not do otherwise' (Moréchand 1968, p.208).

Old Testament prophets could be similarly called against their will. Amos (sixth century BC) was a shepherd called from the desert to prophesy in the prosperous North. The temple priest tried to dismiss him, but Amos complained disarmingly: 'I was no prophet, neither did I belong to any of the brotherhoods of prophets... I was a shepherd, and looked after sycamores, but it was God who took me from herding the flock, and God who said, "Go, prophesy to my people Israel"' (*Amos* 7:1)–16). Amos then proceeded to deliver biting invectives against the opulent, unjust northerners.

Jeremiah's Struggle

The prophet Jeremiah felt called from birth, and struggled against his call:

> The word of the Lord was addressed to me saying,
> 'Before I formed you in the womb I knew you;
> before you came to birth I consecrated you;
> I have appointed you as prophet to the nations' (*Jeremiah* 1:4–10)

Jeremiah pleaded that he was too young and inexperienced for this task:

> I said, 'Ah, Lord God; look, I do not know how to speak: I am a
> child' But the Lord replied:
> 'Do not say "I am a child".
> Go now to those to whom I send you
> and say whatever I command you...'
> Then God put out his hand and touched my mouth
> and said to me:
> 'There! I am putting my words into your mouth' (*Jeremiah* 1:4–10).

From then on, Jeremiah was to be a god-box, a mouthpiece for God. He was hated by those he denounced, and at intervals he tried to abandon his prophetic calling, but his vocation was too powerful for him to resist. In one such crisis of commitment, Jeremiah cries out:

> Woe is me, my mother, for you have borne me
> to be a man of strife and dissension for all the land.
> I neither lend nor borrow, yet all of them curse me.
> Truthfully, God, have I not done my best to serve you?...
> You know I have!
> Do you mean to be for me a deceptive stream
> with inconstant waters?

But God accepted no weakening on Jeremiah's part, and replied to the struggling prophet:

> If you come back,
> I will take you back into my service;
> and if you utter noble, not despicable, thoughts,

> you shall be as my own mouth...
> I am with you to save you and deliver you—
> it is the Lord who speaks (*Jeremiah* 15:10-21).

Like Jeremiah, many shamans receive their call in adolescence. Their call, like Jeremiah's, may be powerful and relentless, and may involve suffering. Yet spiritual leaders are not puppets or pawns of the spiritual world: each makes a free choice to follow their calling. The initial struggle of the shaman against illness or evil marks him out as a wounded healer. He surrenders to chaos and disorder, and through his struggle he learns to master these dangerous forces. He learns to hold on to hope in despair, and reimpose order on chaos. Suffering may invade him, but he learns to challenge and master affliction, becoming a symbol of hope and spiritual power. His initial suffering gives him his vision; the Akawaio Indians say: 'A man must die before he becomes a shaman' (Lewis 1971, pp.70, 188–189).

Wounded Healer

The Old Testament patriarch Jacob was mysteriously wounded in a struggle with spiritual forces after he had stolen his brother's birthright blessing. In this dangerous encounter, Jacob met God face to face: 'Jacob crossed the ford of Jabbok...and there was one that wrestled with him until daybreak who, seeing that he could not master him, struck him on the socket of his hip and Jacob's hip was dislocated as he wrestled with him. He said, "Let me go, for day is breaking". But Jacob answered, "I will not let you go unless you bless me". He then asked, "What is your name?" "Jacob", he replied. He said, "Your name shall no longer be Jacob but Israel; because you have been strong against God, you shall prevail against men". Jacob then made this request, "I beg you, tell me your name," but he replied, "Why do you ask my name?" And he blessed him there. Jacob named the place Peniel, "Because I have seen God face to face," he said, "and I have survived"' (*Genesis* 32:23–32).

The tradition of the wounded healer is strong in Judaeo-Christianity. The book of *Isaiah* describes a suffering servant who would struggle on behalf of many, 'a man of sorrows and familiar with suffering...yet ours were the sufferings he bore' (*Isaiah* 52:13–53:12). Jesus took on this role of suffering to heal others, and many Christians feel they are called to do the same. Through suffering, one becomes familiar with pain, and able to understand the pain of others. Understanding their pain, it becomes possible to help them to grow through it and beyond it. Healing is one of the shaman's important tasks. People go to him or her to be returned to harmony with themselves and with their community, for a shaman can converse with creation and the spirit world.

In 1980 a young Sioux leader came to stay at a centre for Sacred Arts where I was working in Albuquerque, New Mexico. It was his task to perform the mighty prayer of blessing addressed to all creation at the Sioux national gathering that year, but he was disturbed that so many non-believing Americans came to it. He sought permission from his aunt, who was the wise woman of the tribe, to perform the blessing in our dance circle instead. He dressed in his ceremonial robes, and began to chant, stamping gently on the clay floor. He moved round the perimeter of the circle, stopping at the four points of the compass to invoke all of creation, calling them from north, south, east and west. He managed to complete only half the blessing prayer before becoming overwhelmed with exhaustion. He was a healthy man in his mid-twenties, but he explained that he could struggle no further with the forces of evil which he encountered. As it happened, our normally peaceful centre had recently been the scene of considerable violence.

The Healing Group

In many cultures, shamans heal in communal gatherings for prayer, called séances. The community are involved because sickness and misfortune are seen often to be the result of hatred between individuals, families or local communities. The shaman investigates the trouble and tries to relieve both the physical symptoms and the social ills behind them. A parallel in the Catholic Church today would be the communal services of reconciliation which take place in remoter areas of South America, where a catechist may prepare his village for the rare arrival of the priest by leading a day or two of reconciliation, when quarrels are patched up and rivalries are worked through, until all are ready to celebrate Communion together.

Among the Akawaio Indians of British Guiana, who live in small river bank settlements, the shaman analyses the causes of a patient's trouble during a séance. The audience are both witness and judge, for the shaman interprets their opinions. The séance expresses the moral conscience of the community, and the patient has an opportunity to confess his guilt and agree to perform the necessary penance. Harmony is restored, and the shaman delivers his spirit-inspired judgement, based on the consensus of the community (Lewis 1971, pp.159–161). Inuits hold that the greatest danger in their lives is not cold or starvation, but that they have to take the lives of other beings in order to live. Inuit hunters believe they must respect their game, or the animals will not present themselves willingly as a sacrificial offering to the hunter. Inuits maintain equilibrium between themselves and the spirit world by a host of behavioural codes and taboos; when these are broken, they must be forgiven (Brown 1985, p.397). An Inuit séance recorded by Rasmussen resembles a modern analytic group therapy session, except for the audience's repeated refrain of 'Let her be forgiven'. An important part of healing is forgiveness, as the Catholic Church recognises in its sacrament of Confession.

The shaman begins his diagnosis: 'I ask you, my helping spirit, whence comes the illness from which this person is suffering... Is it brought about by the sick woman herself? Is she herself the cause of the disease?' The woman replies: 'The sickness is due to my own fault. I have ill-fulfilled my duties. My thoughts have been bad and my actions evil'. The shaman suggests: 'There is something that gleams white. It is the edge of a pipe, or what can it be?' The audience chime in helpfully: 'She has smoked a pipe that she ought not to have smoked. But never mind. We will not take any notice of that. Let her be forgiven'.

But the shaman persists: 'That is not all. There are other offences which have brought about this disease. Is it due to me or to the sick person herself?' The patient responds: 'It is due to myself alone. There was something the matter with my abdomen, with my inside'. The shaman suggests: 'She has split a meat bone which she ought not to have touched'. The audience plead: 'Let her be released from her offence!' but the shaman pursues his search: 'She is not released from her evil. It is dangerous, It is a matter for anxiety. Helping spirit, say what it is that plagues her!' The séance may continue for hours, and further sessions may follow, until the patient seems thoroughly purged, and on the road to recovery (Rasmussen 1929, p.133).

Spiritual Marriage

How do shamans describe their relationship with God? In some tribes, such as the Tungus of North Asia, the shaman is bound by a contract to the divinity he worships, as Catholic priests and nuns bind themselves to God by vow. Shamans have an intimate connection with the spiritual world, and may express this in terms of a love relationship. Some shamans describe their union as a spiritual marriage, a concept found in many religions. St. Paul told his new converts that he had wedded them to Christ, and mystics such as St. Bernard (twelfth century) wrote of Christ as his soul's bridegroom. Nuns understand themselves to be wedded to Christ, and similar concepts are found in Islam. In Ethiopia, a woman shaman novice is called a'bride' and is assigned two best men who will help her if she has difficulties with her spiritual husband (Lewis 1971, p.57–63).

Japanese women shamans in Yamashiro are blind, perhaps because blindness is thought to heighten inner sight. The senior shaman normally has four or five apprentices. Before their initiation, the novices live in isolation. They fast, purify themselves, put on a white shroud and eat the food of the dead, as a sign of their death to the world. They pound rice with a pestle and mortar until it turns to a stiff paste. The simple activity of pounding rice for days on end gradually focuses their energy until they fall into a trance. Each novice then spends a week in the shrine room of her clan's deity. If she is called into his service, she is married to the spirit who appeared to her during her trance. She brings a dowry of a cooking pot for rice, a frying pan and other household utensils, as she would into a normal marriage. Formerly, a temple priest would stand in for the god of the clan, and marry and have intercourse with her (Eder 1958, pp.367–380).

In the voodoo cults of Haiti, women may enter into a heavenly marriage in which they are given a ring and a wedding certificate. The following is a certificate recording the heavenly marriage of Madame Cétoute with her spirit partner who is named Damballah:

> 'Republic of Haiti. The year 1949 and 6th day of the month of January at 3pm. We, Jean Jumeau, Registrar of Port-au-Prince, signify that citizens Damballah Toquan Miroissé and Madame Andrémise Cétoute appeared before us to be united by the indissoluble bond of the marriage sacrament. Inasmuch as Madame Cétoute must consecrate Tuesday and Thursday to her husband Damballah without ever a blemish on herself, it being understood Monsieur Damballah's duty is to load his wife with good luck so that Madame Cétoute will never know a day's poverty: the husband Monsieur Damballah is accountable to his wife and owes her all necessary protection as set down in the contract. It is with work that spiritual and material property is amassed. In execution of article 15.1 of the Haitian Code. They hereto agreed in the affirmative before qualified witnesses whose names are given'. Their signatures follow (Métraux 1959, p.215).

Voodoo developed from Christian roots, and Madame Cétoute's contract is not so far removed from a nun's vow chart which she signs on her profession day in the presence of church officials. She too promises to live 'without ever a blemish', and a representative of the Church puts a ring on her finger as a sign of her indissoluble bond. When an English Benedictine nun makes her solemn vows, she reads out the following:

> 'In the name of our Lord Jesus Christ. Amen. In the year of our Lord N..., I, Sister N... in the county of N... in the diocese of N... in England promise for life before God and his saints, stability, conversion of life and obedience,... under the Right Reverend N..., Abbess of the monastery of N... and her successors,... in the presence of the Right Reverend N..., Abbess, and the community of the same monastery. In witness whereof I have hereunto set my hand, in the year, month and day aforesaid'. She signs the document, as does the abbess and also the abbot who presides over the monasteries of Britain.

Trance

A spiritual union enshrined in such a document can be powerful and deep. Its closest human parallel, perhaps, is sexual union. A Jewish rabbi said: 'Prayer is a coupling with the glory of God'. Spirit-filled men and women of different ages and cultures have struggled to find words to describe their experience of union with God. The Spanish Carmelite friar John of the Cross (fifteenth century) spoke of Christ as his beloved spouse, and when God seemed absent, the friar described the experience as a searing dark night. Intense prayer is experienced in most cultures as ecstasy—an overwhelming sense of being drawn beyond oneself. Bernini's sculpture of St. Teresa of Avila in ecstasy portrays her falling backwards in trance, her mouth open and her eyes shut, as her senses are drawn into the world beyond.

Recording his visions, St. Paul's comment on how he perceived them was 'whether in or out of the body, I do not know' (2 *Corinthians* 12:2). The human body goes into trance when its normal faculties are suspended and attention is withdrawn from one's immediate environment. Christian charismatics at prayer lose control of their bodies and fall back into the arms of waiting helpers, an action they describe as being 'slain in the Spirit'. Shamans, who normally fall into trance, may describe their spiritual possession as a 'half death' or 'little death', as they die to their external environment and live to the spirit world. The sexual parallel is clear.

In this chapter, I have purposely refrained from describing the more strange and fantastic aspects of shamans' life and behaviour. Instead I have focused on the qualities which shamans share with spiritual leaders in other cultures, particularly Judaeo-Christianity. Any religious tradition appears strange to outsiders, including the variety of Christian traditions. In cultures where the shaman is a normal part of life, Christianity must appear strange and fantastic. Yet the shaman's call, his function and his way of life are not so far removed from those of the Christian priest. Both lead their people to heaven through prayer and holiness. Prayer is difficult to classify in our post-Christian western world, but it forms the basis of the life of both priest and shaman, and it is through their praying that they share a common sense of the sacred, and become for their people a symbol of God.

CHAPTER 9

Chant and Incantation
Sacred Song

The psalms were the favourite prayer chants of the ancient Jews and, until recently, Christian monks and nuns chanted these 150 sacred songs every week. Members of strict religious orders spend more time chanting than they spend speaking to one another. As a young adult, I spent four years in a monastery in which the community gathers five times a day to chant psalms. Chanting is a powerful form of bonding with a group and with God. For years after leaving the monastery, I felt stripped of the powerful experience of chanting.

Chant: A Two-Way Symbol

Chant, or ritual song, is perhaps the most complex symbol in this book. Our song symbolises ourself. When we pray in song, we bring our deeper self to God. St. Augustine (fifth century) wrote: 'He who sings, prays twice'. Song is a way to carry our thoughts and feelings out of ourselves towards God. A holy song is also a symbol of God: it embodies God's message to us. A song which conveys God's life is full of power. It may be difficult for Christians to imagine that, for example, American Indian chants can heal and bring life, but this is perhaps because Christians no longer expect to receive life through their own holy songs.

Near Eastern peoples accompanied their chants on the lyre or kithara. In many mythologies, the gods taught people the art of music. The ancient Egyptians held that the god of Wisdom, Thot, invented the lyre. The ancient Greeks taught that the god Apollo was the first to play the kithara. The early Saivite Hindu sect believed that the god Shiva created music, dance and drama, and gave them to us. The ancient Vaishnavites, also in India, taught that Lord Krishna invented music by playing a reed pipe, and charmed wild animals and reptiles with his music (Puthanangady p.178, n.2). These myths are the attempts of various peoples to explain the divine power they experienced through music.

The Music of Creation

Ancient peoples were very aware of the sounds they heard in the natural world around them: birdsong, animal calls, the ocean's roar. Ancient Jewish psalms picture trees, rivers and seas singing to God:

> Let the heavens rejoice and earth be glad,
> let the sea and all within it thunder praise,
> let the land and all it bears rejoice,
> all the trees of the wood shout for joy (*Psalm* 95:11,12).

> Let the rivers clap their hands
> and the hills ring out their joy
> at the presence of the Lord (*Psalm* 97:8).

The Israelites who wrote this poetry delighted in the world around them in the same way as the American Indians who chanted:

> You whose day it is, make it beautiful.
> Get out your rainbow colours,
> so it will be beautiful (Astrov 1962, p.279).

And:

> The bush is sitting
> under a tree
> and singing (Cronyn 1918).

Earliest Chants

The music of archaic peoples is utilitarian, with magical, symbolic or social functions. It is more than entertainment, and is treated with reverence. For many peoples, the voice of the priest or the sound of an instrument is a medium for the voice of the Creator. Since both voice and instruments have ritual and symbolic value, a performer must use predetermined sounds and techniques. Strange sounds produced with rattles, clappers or friction drums may be used to repel or personify evil spirits, in the same way that the 'noise of darkness' became part of Holy Week services in parts of Europe. Until recently, church bells fell silent for the three days before Easter, and clappers replaced them until the Gloria on Easter night, when Christ's resurrection was celebrated. Ancient Egyptians repelled evil spirits with the sistrum, small bells attached to a metal disc. Armenian and Syrian Christians still shake the sistrum in their Holy Week services.

From early times, most human activities were associated with music, and chants were sung to ensure blessing. The song to the oxen in southern France is one of many European and Arab songs for tilling the soil. These are ornate chants with free rhythms delivered at full voice into space, which may be punctuated by exhortations shouted to the animals (Hindley 1981, pp.17–18). Aborigine peoples use music in a variety of ways. Their 'clever-men' become shamans in their twenties, and use songs in much of their work. They sing patients into a receptive state, and chant evil out of their patients' bodies. They believe this to be the most successful way to soothe and heal them. A clever-man can sing an enemy to blindness or even death by chanting evil songs. When there is drought, the men sing rain chants. The Kurnai of Gippsland squirt water in the direction from which they expect rain and sing rain chants received in dreams by their men and women. There are other ceremonies to stop rain if it continues too long. At a death, women wail and all sing special songs (McCarthy 1957, pp.149–152).

Ancient Israelites used all these kinds of holy chants. They called them 'NGN', a word meaning 'to intone or cast a spell upon; to sing with a purpose'. The nasal sound of this Hebrew word is the basis of our word chant, and also of enchant, enchanter, incantation and similar words. Water was as essential to

20. *Ancient Egyptian enchanting with his hand, accompanying his incantation on the harp.*
(*Drawing by Margaret Rees, from a wall painting at Thebes*)

these Israelites as it is to the Aborigines, and so the prophet Elisha (ninth century BC) called for a musician to chant for water. He ordered: '"Now bring me someone who can play the lyre!" And as the musician played, the hand of the Lord was laid on him, and he said, "the Lord says this, 'Dig ditch on ditch in this wadi,' for the Lord says, you shall see neither wind nor rain, but this wadi shall be filled with water, and you and your troops and your baggage animals shall drink"' (2 *Kings* 3:15–17) (Wulstan 1968).

Healing Chants

Israelites used chants to soothe the sick and remove evil from them, as do the Aborigines. King Saul (tenth century BC) sent for the young David to soothe him and release him from the grip of an evil spirit. David accompanied his incantations on the harp or, as the Hebrew puts it, 'he enchanted with his hand'. The author of the First Book of *Samuel* writes: 'The Spirit of the Lord had left Saul, and an evil spirit from the Lord filled him with terror. Saul's servants said to him, "Look, an evil spirit of God is the cause of your terror. Let our lord give the order, and your servants who wait on you will look for a skilled harpist; when the evil spirit of God troubles you, the harpist will play and you will recover".' David was sent for, and the account concludes: 'Whenever the spirit from God troubled Saul, David took the harp and played, and then Saul grew calm and recovered, and the evil spirit left him' (1 *Samuel* 16:14–23) (Wulstan 1968) .

Healing chants were used in Israel into Christian times. One of the Qumran psalm scrolls says 'he sang songs over the sick'. The apostle James encouraged Christian elders to care for their sick by anointing them with oil in God's name and praying over them (*James* 5:14, 15). Today, charismatics in many Christian churches pray for their sick by placing their hands on them and chanting over them. People of every culture have recognised music's healing potential; Renaissance instrument tutor books extol the healing powers of music which their students will, it is hoped, soon master. Thomas Mace (1966, p.31) writes:

> This art (music) excelleth all without control;
> The faculties it moveth of the soul:
> It stifles wrath, it causes griefs to cease,
> It doth excite the furious mind to peace
> (*Musick's Monument*, 1676).

Chants of Destruction

We may be either dubious or shocked that Aborigines sing people to blindness or even to death by chanting evil songs, yet this was a widespread concept in the ancient world. In the Book of *Job* (fifth century BC), its hero complains that the men who formerly looked up to him now chant songs against him (*Job* 30:9). The author of the *Lamentations of Jeremiah* (fourth century BC) complains that his enemies do the same: 'Our enemies have opened their mouths in chorus against us' (*Lamentations* 2:16; 3:46). It may seem far-fetched to believe that chanting can kill, yet some animals kill their enemies by emitting high-pitched notes. Hawks paralyse their prey by shrieking, much as Japanese samurai use a scream, pitched at a certain level, to paralyse their opponents (Kalweit 1988, p.159).

Chanting was an ancient tactic for success in battle. War was a holy thing for ancient peoples: you fought to defend the territory of your god, to preserve your sacred space against the intruding forces of chaos. The Israelites fought and chanted in this way:

> Let the praise of God be on their lips
> and a two-edged sword in their hands,
> deal out vengeance to the nations
> and punishment on all the peoples...
> to carry out the sentence pre-ordained:
> this honour is for all his faithful (*Psalm* 149:5–9).

We possess some interesting accounts of the war chants of the early Israelites. Gideon (11th century BC) attacked the Midianites and other eastern tribes amassed against Israel, with 300 men who chanted their holy shout, 'The sword of the Lord and of Gideon!', and blew their trumpets and smashed their pitchers as a shattering accompaniment (*Judges* 7:16–22). When he reached the walls of Jericho, Joshua ordered the priests to blow their trumpets, 'and when the army heard the trumpet sound, they raised a great shout, and down fell the walls' (*Joshua* 6:20). Modern technology no longer allows time for battle cries, but still today, at important moments in her worship, the Catholic Church chants a litany, in which a leader names a succession of holy people one by one, and the congregation responds 'Pray for us!' after each invocation. This litany possibly developed from that chanted by Roman soldiers before engaging in battle (Jungmann 1960, p.25). The Christian community chants a litany on Easter night and at other times when it baptises new members, as it defies the kingdom of darkness and claims new children for the kingdom of God.

Shamans Receive Songs

Who invented the ancient chants which were so powerful that they caused death, or life and healing? In many early cultures, shamans received these songs and shared them with their people. A shaman's song arose from his deep experience of the spirit world. He embodied spiritual powers as he sang, and so his song was powerful. Music and song are ancient means of bringing people into harmony with themselves, their environment and the whole of creation, and shamans understood this. A shaman's song is central to who he is and what he does. His song is not merely about life; it conveys life: it is a symbol which contains power.

Many shamans received their call through their song, and anthropologists have recorded accounts of how Siberian shamans did so. A Siberian shaman named Kokuiev struggled for three years against the songs that welled up inside him. He had continuous headaches as a result of trying to ignore the songs. Sometimes he would chant them in his sleep, and then he would feel better for a few days. Eventually, he gave up struggling against his songs, and became a shaman. The anthropologist Diószegi recorded his story: 'I also became ill when I was about to become a shaman... I had been ailing for about three years. In the meantime, the spirits came to visit me. While I slept, my tongue was chanting. It chanted like shamans do. But I did not know anything about it. When I awoke, my mother and father and my sister told me "You were chanting shaman songs"... It went on like this... One keeps suffering and suffering. When you want to rest or sleep, your tongue would be chanting... When I had no more strength left to suffer, finally I agreed to become a shaman. And when I became a shaman, I changed entirely. Because being a shaman turns one into quite a different person' (Diószegi 1968, p.142 ff.).

Joyful Healing Songs

An Igulik Inuit shaman named Avá–Nembiará learnt his song in solitude. He would move through sadness and weeping into great joy which was so power-ful that he had to sing. The anthropologist Rasmussen recorded him saying: 'Then I sought solitude, and here I soon became very melancholy... Then, for no reason, all would suddenly be changed, and I felt a great, inexplicable joy, a joy so powerful that I could not restrain it, but had to break into song, a mighty song with only room for one word: joy, joy! And I had to use the full strength of my voice. And then, in the midst of such a fit of mysterious and overwhelming delight, I became a shaman, not knowing myself how it came about. But I was a shaman. I could see and hear in a totally different way' (Rasmussen 1930, p.118).

Rasmussen recorded another story of an Inuit woman shaman named Uvavnuk. One winter evening, out in the open, she felt that she had been struck by a ball of fire and was filled with joy. She ran home and started to sing. Her song filled others with joy, and healed them of malice. Another shaman told Rasmussen what happened: 'One evening she had gone out to pass water. It was a dark winter evening, and suddenly a shining ball of fire showed in the sky. It came down to earth directly toward the place where Uvavnuk sat. She wanted to run away, but before she could do so, she was struck by the ball of fire. She became aware all at once that everything in her began to glow. She lost consciousness, and from that moment on, was a great summoner of spirits... Uvavnuk came running into the house, half unconscious, and sang a song which since then has become her magic formula whenever she has to help others. As soon as she began to sing, she became delirious with joy, and all the others in the house were also beyond themselves with joy, because their minds were being cleansed of all that burdened them. They lifted up their arms and cast away everything connected with suspicion and malice' (Rasmussen 1927, p.34). Uvav-nuk's song was one of union with creation and its power: the great sea, river currents, the open sky and the powerful storm. This is the song she received:

> The great sea has set me in motion,
> set me adrift,
> moving me as the weed moves in a river.
> The arch of the sky and mightiness of storms
> have moved the spirit within me,
> till I am carried away,
> trembling with joy (Rasmussen 1927, p.34).

21. *An eskimo woman sings an incantation with her magic breath. (After a stonecut/stencil by Myra Kukiiyat, 1971, in Winnipeg Art Gallery)*

Songs are Powerful Thoughts

Another Inuit, Orpingalik, explained how his songs came: songs are thoughts which are too powerful merely to be spoken. They contain the same power as do floods and ice floes: 'Songs are thoughts sung out with the breath when people are moved by great forces, and ordinary speech no longer suffices. Man is moved just like an ice floe sailing here and there out in the current… Thought can wash over him like a flood, making his breath come in gasps and his heart throb'. Then Orpingalik uses a beautiful phrase to describe how the awestruck singer is filled with yet deeper awe: 'Then it will happen that we, who always think that we are small, will feel still smaller. And we will fear to use words. But it will happen that the words we need will come of themselves. When the words we want to use shoot up of themselves—we get a new song' (Rasmussen 1931, p.321).

The prophets of ancient Israel described their call in various ways, some in language similar to that of the Siberian shamans. Isaiah (eighth century BC) felt set on fire with a heavenly coal, with which an angel touched his lips, much as the Siberian woman Uvavnuk was struck by fire when she received her song: 'I saw the Lord God seated on a high throne...the temple was filled with smoke... Then one of the seraphs flew to me, holding in his hand a live coal which he had taken from the altar with a pair of tongs. With this he touched my mouth and said: "See now, this has touched your lips"' (*Isaiah* 6:1–7). Isaiah then embarked on a lifetime of preaching, delivering oracles and chanting songs of unrivalled beauty and power.

In some cultures, any member of the tribe can seek a vision or a sacred song. If you were a Papago Indian male, you could do so through a fierce battle, by killing an eagle, or by making the arduous four-day pilgrimage southwards from the desert to the Gulf of California. If you were a woman, you could contact higher powers and gain access to hidden inner resources through withdrawal and fasting for four days during menstruation. Ancient Israelites used some of these means to encounter God. The prophet Elijah (ninth century BC) walked for forty days into the desert in order to experience God (1 *Kings* 19:8), and the gospels picture Jesus fasting for forty days in the desert before returning to his people to begin his healing work. As with the American Indians, everyone could sing sacred chants and, in ancient Israel, the 150 psalms were the chief collection of such holy songs.

David's Chants

The psalms evolved over many centuries, although King David (tenth century BC) has traditionally been credited as their composer. As we have seen, as a young man, David used his chanting skills to cast out Saul's evil spirit. The book of *Ecclesiasticus* (second century BC), drawn up centuries after David's death, describes him putting his heart into his sacred songs:

> He put all his heart into his songs
> out of love for his Maker.
> He placed harps before the altar
> to make the singing sweeter with their music;
> he gave the feasts their splendour,
> the festivals their solemn pomp (*Ecclesiasticus* 47:8, 9).

The measured tone of this account indicates that by this time, sacred chanting had become rather institutionalised. A more enthusiastic description of how it felt to lead the community in sacred song is found in a psalm written when the Jews were in exile in the eighth century BC, and keenly felt the loss of their holy task:

> These things will I remember
> as I pour out my soul:
> how I would lead the rejoicing crowd
> into the house of God
> amid cries of gladness and thanksgiving,
> the throng wild with joy! (*Psalm* 41:5).

The temple liturgy included both inspired prophetic chanting and fixed musical forms, with a large choir and orchestra. A chronicler of the third century BC gives us an account of worship in King David's temple, although he is probably describing the liturgy of his own time: 'For the liturgy, David and the senior officers set apart...prophets who accompanied themselves with lyre and harp and cymbal, and a list was made of those with these duties to perform... There were six sons of Jeduthun under the direction of their father Jeduthun who, to the sound of the lyre, prophesied to the glory and praise of the Lord... Sons of Herman, the king's seer, sounded the trumpet to accompany God's words... God gave Herman fourteen sons and three daughters; all of them sang in the temple of the Lord under their father's direction, to the sound of cymbal, harp and lyre, for the liturgy of the house of the Lord... Those who had learned to sing to the Lord were registered with their kinsmen; the total of those so trained was 288. Junior and senior, master and pupil alike, they drew lots for their term of duty' (1 *Chronicles* 25:1–9). The temple liturgy must have been colourful.

A Hermit's Song

In the Christian West, civilisation grew increasingly complex, but in fourteenth century Yorkshire, the hermit Richard Rolle described his call and his song in language similar to that of the Inuit shamans. Richard ran away from home to become a hermit, making a rough and ready habit out of his father's rainhood and two of his sister's frocks. He became an influential writer, and was spiritual director to the Cistercian nuns at Hampole near Doncaster when he died at the age of 49. He described his call as a sense of being struck with fire and set aglow. He wrote:'I cannot tell you how surprised I was the first time I felt my heart begin to warm. It was real warmth too, not imaginary, and it felt as if it were actually on fire... I had to keep feeling my breast, to make sure there was no physical reason for it!... It set my soul aglow as if a real fire were burning there' (Rolle 1972, p.45).

Richard described how his inner fire welled up into song: 'A man overflows with inner joy, and his very thought sings as he rejoices in the warmth of his love... Once a man has known some such experience, he is never thereafter wholly without it, for there always remains a sort of glow, some song or sweetness,...unless illness catches him, or he is gripped by intolerable hunger or thirst, or is held up by cold, or heat, or travel' (Rolle 1972, p.77). Like the shaman Kokuiev, his tongue kept chanting unless he was in pain and like Avá-Nembiará he learnt his song in solitude: 'I used to delight indeed to sit alone, so that away from all the racket, my song could flow more easily' (Rolle 1972, p.148). Like Orpingalik, Richard explained that his songs were thoughts too powerful to speak, welling up from his inner joy: 'My thinking itself turned into melodious song, and my meditation became a poem, and my very prayers and psalms took up the same sound. The effect of this inner sweetness was that I began to sing what previously I had spoken' (Rolle 1972, p.93).

The Creative Word

Song is heightened speech, and holy songs are heightened prayers. Why do shamans tell us that these prayers are so powerful? The answer is that early cultures believed in the power of the word. Our wordy culture has debased this concept: we litter our lives with words but, in earlier cultures, words grew out of silence. A true word does not fall to the ground unheeded: it evokes a response. For the ancient Israelites, words were holy, and to be used with care and responsibility. A word has an effect as inevitable as the growth of corn after rain, declared the prophet Isaiah, speaking in God's name: 'Yes, as the rain and the snow come down from the heavens and do not return without watering the earth, making it yield and giving growth to provide seed for the sower and bread for the eating, so the word that goes forth from my mouth does not return to me empty, without carrying out my will and succeeding in what it was sent to do' (*Isaiah* 55:10, 11).

American Indians have a deep understanding of the power of the word. In their culture, each person can receive a holy song as a gift through a dream or intuition, or through the ascetic discipline of watching and fasting, which opens him or her more deeply to the supernatural. His song has creative power to heal, to ward off evil or to bring forth life. Christians sing hymns without necessarily expecting a response. In 'The Lord's my shepherd' we sing:

> He leadeth me
> The quiet waters by.
> My soul he doth restore again.

Yet we do not really expect our soul to be restored through our song. American Indians expect their songs to be effective. The Yuma Indians of California sing this song to heal someone suffering from depression:

> Your heart is good.
> Shining darkness will be here.
> You think only of sad, unpleasant things;

you are to think of goodness.
Lie down and sleep here.
Shining darkness will join us.
You think of this goodness in your dream.
Goodness will be given to you.
I will speak for it, and it will come to pass.
It will happen here,
I will ask for your good.
It will happen as I sit by you,
It will be done as I sit here in this place (Astrov 1962, p.265).

Chant for a Lame Person

The Navajo Indians of the Southwest chant this prayer for someone whose legs are injured, who wants to walk again:

O God! Your offering I make.
I have prepared a smoke for you.
Restore my feet for me.
Restore my legs for me.
Restore my body for me.
Restore my mind for me.
This very day take out your spell for me.
Your spell remove for me.
You have taken it away for me.
Far off it has gone.
Happily I recover.

Happily my interior becomes cool.
Happily I go forth.
My interior feeling cool, may I walk.
No longer sore, may I walk.
Impervious to pain, may I walk.
With lively feelings may I walk.

Happily may I walk.
Happily, with abundant dark clouds, may I walk.
Happily, with abundant showers, may I walk.
Happily, with abundant plants, may I walk.
Happily, on a trail of pollen, may I walk.
Happily may I walk.
Being as it used to be long ago, may I walk.

May it be beautiful before me.
May it be beautiful behind me.
May it be beautiful below me.
May it be beautiful above me.
May it be beautiful all around me.
In beauty it is finished (Astrov 1962, pp.185–186).

In other songs, the singer wrestles with the problem of evil or with the question of death. Sometimes death must be faced, struggled with and calmly accepted; sometimes life may return. Sometimes the patient must walk forward through death into something unknown. The Luiseno Indians of California sing this song to accept death:

> At the time of death,
> When I found there was to be death,
> I was very much surprised.
> All was failing.
> My home,
> I was sad to leave it.
>
> I have been looking far,
> sending my spirit north, south, east and west,
> trying to escape from death,
> but could find nothing,
> no way of escape (Astrov 1962, p.262).

Celtic Binding Chants

For many centuries, Celtic Christians retained a belief in the power of their chants. We have inherited many Celtic binding songs, in which the singer 'binds himself' to the power of Christ for protection against evil. Some of these are versions of St. Patrick's Breastplate, of which the original is attributed to St. Patrick (fifth century AD). These chants develop St. Paul's image of the Christian putting on the armour of Christ to make himself strong (Ephesians 6:13–17). One early medieval breastplate chant is more specific than most:

> Christ's cross over this face, and thus over my ear. Christ's
> cross over this eye. Christ's cross over this nose.
> Christ's cross to accompany me before. Christ's cross to
> accompany behind me. Christ's cross to meet every difficulty,
> both on hollow and hill.
> Christ's cross eastward facing me. Christ's cross back
> towards the sunset. In the north, in the south, increasingly may
> Christ's cross straightway be...
> Christ's cross over me as I sit. Christ's cross over me as
> I lie. Christ's cross be all my strength until we reach the King of
> heaven.
> From the top of my head to the nail of my foot, O Christ,
> against every danger I trust in the protection of the cross.
> (Murphy 1956, pp.33–34).

A crofter on the island of Barra in the Hebrides sang the following binding chant, in which he called on Christ to shield and encircle him:

> My Christ! My Christ! My shield, my encircler,
> Each day, each night, each light, each dark.

Be near me, uphold me, my treasure, my triumph,
In my lying, in my standing, in my watching, in my sleeping.

Jesus, son of Mary! My helper, my encircler,
Jesus, son of David, my strength everlasting.
                                    (Carmichael 1900, vol.3, p.77).

The Medieval Modes
Medieval Christians gradually lost their belief in the power of their chants. They codified them according to eight scales or *modes*, as did the ancient Israelites before them. Since the Hebrew meaning of the word *mode* was to sing with a purpose, the original Hebrew modes were not scales but collections of sacred songs or incantations. Each mode was used for a specific purpose, and so had its own indefinable ethos. Most chants sharing this ethos would make use of the same note-patterns, and in time, theorists came to define modes in terms of scale structure. When the Christian Church adopted the chants of the Jews, it inherited the modes, each with its indefinable ethos, similarity of note-patterns and special scale structure. But ethos was the most important characteristic of a mode (Wulstan 1968).

What this ethos was, wherein lay this similarity of note-patterns, or how the scale was constructed, was relatively insignificant. When the Flemish monk and theorist, Hucbald (c. 849–930) cleverly added the ancient Greek names to the Latin modes, he inadvertently named them in descending rather than ascending order. In this way, the Greek 'Phrygian' (or 'warlike') mode became Hucbald's 'Dorian' (or 'D') mode. Yet Hucbald's names stuck, for the medieval musician had sufficient imagination to enjoy any allusion, however remote. Like those of earlier cultures, medieval musicians felt it imperative to keep the idea of modes, or categories of sacred song, however little these categories might correspond to the sacred chants themselves. Gradually, however, theorists subjected the melodies to a rigorous procrustean treatment. Irregular chants were suppressed, altered or transposed. Abbot Odo of Cluny (d. 942) describes a mode as a pattern to which tunes can be made to fit by the musician who first 'goes through all the modes to determine whether the melody may perhaps not stand in one or another... If it suits no mode, let it be emended according to the one with which it least disagrees' (Strunk (i) 1981, pp.32–33). Yet Hucbald preserved melodies in a special notation he had devised which show chromaticisms not found in later regularised chants (Wulstan 1968).

The Modes Break Down
In the later middle ages, composers began to break away from modal patterns, but felt it necessary to keep up a pretence of following the sacred modes. They began to use hitherto forbidden sharps and flats, and invented a clef code, whereby a singer's line of music might be transposed to avoid dreaded black

notes. The note 'B' was avoided for centuries. The Carolingian renaissance led to the proliferation and embellishment of church music. Through the enthusiasm of the Benedictine and especially of the Cluniac monks, every type of text and chant was prolonged without restraint. Worship was now performed round the clock by shifts of monks, and composers were busy writing tropes and sequences, alleluia and offertory verses, neums and jubili, antiphons and responsories.

In the first half of the twelfth century, a reaction grew in the Cistercian monasteries. Chant acquired a new soberness, and by the fourteenth century it was brought back to reasonable proportions. But the Cistercians also made less fortunate emendations: they transposed passages to make chants obey the rules of the theorists, and even pruned passages which exceeded a range of ten notes through a misunderstanding of the psalm verse, 'Sing him songs on the ten-stringed lute' (*Psalm* 143:9).

The concept of modes or sacred songs lasted into the sixteenth century, when the modes were gradually superseded by the major and minor scales which we use today. The Flemish composer Josquin composed a setting of the psalm *De Profundis* ('Out of the depths') which the sixteenth century Swiss monk Glareanus clumsily described using the language of the modes. He writes that the music 'creeps...without offending the ear from the Dorian to the Phrygian' and 'ends the combined systems of the Dorian and the Hypodorian on 'E', the seat of the Phrygian'. He adds: 'the motet remains between 'A' and 'D', respecting the limits of the Dorian and Hypodorian systems' (Strunk (ii) 1981, pp.32–33). Glareanus is here using the language of the modes to describe concepts which could be explained more simply in terms of key and tonality. The theorists had finally become entangled by their theories.

Song in the Reformed Churches

But sacred song remained. In the new Reformed Churches, most symbols were discarded, but music was highly prized as a symbol both of our heart's worship and of God's healing power. In *Pilgrim's Progress* by John Bunyan (1675), Christian often breaks into holy song: 'Then Christian gave three leaps for joy and went on singing, "Thus far did I come, laden with my sin"...' (Bunyan 1951, part 1, p.30). Christian and Hopeful 'went softly along the right way, singing: "Come hither, you that walk along the way"...' (Bunyan 1951, part 1, p.94). In a quaint passage, John Bunyan even indicates that we join in the sacred song of all creation, by describing how the birds sing holy chants:

> Christiana thought she heard in a grove, a little way off on the right hand, a most curious melodious note, with words much like these:
>
> > 'Through all my life, thy favour is
> > So frankly shown to me,

That in thy house for evermore
My dwelling place shall be'...

So Christiana asked Prudence who it was that made these curious notes. 'They are,' she answered, 'our country birds: they sing these notes but seldom, except it be at the Spring... I often,' said she, 'go out to hear them;...they make the woods and groves and solitary places desirous to be in' (Bunyan 1951, part 2, p.169).

As Wesley toured the English countryside and towns, he gave people a new experience of the creative power of the word of God. The words of scripture came alive for his converts, and they expressed their response through singing the new Wesleyan hymns. They also learnt to point, or chant, the psalms. Later, when the Reformed tradition in its turn tended to become wordy and long drawn out in style, a new wave of Pentecostal Churches rediscovered the power of praying and chanting to heal and give life. Today, charismatic (or 'power-bearing') songs are a feature of most Christian Churches. The powerful but elusive symbol of holy chant is still alive.

CHAPTER 10

The Dance of Heaven and Earth

The Dance of Creation

> I danced in the morning when the world was begun
> And I danced in the moon and the stars and the sun;
> I came down from heaven and I danced on the earth;
> At Bethlehem I had my birth.
> Dance, then, wherever you may be;
> I am the Lord of the Dance, said he,
> And I'll lead you all wherever you may be,
> And I'll lead you all in the dance, said he (Carter 1963).

In this contemporary hymn, Sydney Carter describes Christ as Lord of the dance of creation. Other myths describe the creation of the world as the dance of God. In India, Shiva is Lord of the dance. He awakens matter by sending waves of sound through it, and matter dances, appearing around him as an aureole of flames. He tramples Asura, the demon of ignorance, as he dances the five-fold dance of creation, veiling, preservation, destruction and release. He performs his dance both at the centre of the universe and within the worshipper's heart. In India, dance is intimately related to worship; carvings and paintings of heavenly dancers adorn hundreds of temples. In Hindu village communities, the actors of dance-rituals fulfil the role of priests, as they mediate the divine to their people (Barnes 1991, p.46). Temple dancers were dedicated as servants of God at an early age, and led austere lives to perform their sacred task. Indian dancers follow ancient traditions and use their whole body to reflect the life and beauty of the universe.

The author of the book of *Genesis* describes God creating the universe in a rhythmic sequence, day by day, like a dance, and the author of the book of Job describes God asking:

> Where were you when I laid the earth's foundation...
> while the morning stars sang together
> and all the angels shouted for joy? (*Job* 38:4–7).

Psalm 19 describes the powerful, yet silent, dance of the heavens around their creator:

22. **Indian women dancing with lights, from an Indian batik.** *(Drawing by Sr. Regina, Turvey Abbey)*

> The heavens declare the glory of God;
> the skies proclaim the work of his hands.
> Day after day they pour forth their speech;
> night after night they display their knowledge...
> Their voice goes out into all the earth,
> their words to the utmost bounds of the world (*Psalm* 19:1–4).

Shakespeare depicts the circling stars in a sentence:

> There's not the smallest orb which thou behold'st
> But in his motion like an angel sings.
> > (Lorenzo, in *The Merchant of Venice*, 1594–6).

Earthly Dance

For the Greeks, song was related to dance. The word 'choir' (Greek: 'chorea') means a singing and dancing chorus. Lucian of Samosata (third century) speaks beautifully of dance: it 'brings the souls of people into the right rhythm, and reveals what the inner beauty of the soul has in common with the outer beauty of the body, because it shows the point where the two flow into one another'. Dance 'proclaims what is in the mind, and makes manifest what is unseen' (Rahner (ii) 1963, pp.68–69). Then the writer's imagination soars as he places dancing humanity in a cosmic setting: the origin of dance 'is the same as that of the world itself, and it appeared with the love that is the beginning of all, for the dance of the stars, the intertwining of the planets, the common measure and sweet harmony of their movements are all repetitions of the great dance that was in the beginning' (Rahner (ii) 1963, pp.71–72). As late as 1589, Arbeau concluded his dance manual by urging his readers: 'Meanwhile, practise these dances thoroughly, and make yourself a worthy companion to the planets, who are natural dancers' (Arbeau 1967, p.195).

In the Old Testament, dance featured prominently, especially during the chief annual festivals, when Jews gathered to celebrate their sacred history. At least eight varieties of dance are described, the most common being a whirling movement (Hebrew: 'hul'), and another being a skipping, leaping movement (Hebrew: 'raqad')(Long 1976, p.19). When the Israelites escaped across the Red Sea, Miriam the prophetess and her attendants danced in triumph, accompanied by timbrels and song (*Exodus* 15:20, 21). Jephthah's daughter danced to the timbrel (*Judges* 11:34). *Ecclesiastes* speaks of 'a time to mourn and a time to dance' (*Ecclesiastes* 3:4). In Matthew's gospel, Jesus quotes a children's song: 'We played the flute for you (as at a wedding) and you did not dance; we sang a dirge to you (as at a funeral) and you did not mourn' (*Matthew* 11:17). Singing accompanied dancing. Psalm 149 urges the people:

> Sing a new song to the Lord...
> Let the people of Zion be glad in their King.

Let them praise his name with dancing,
and make music to him with timbrel and harp (*Psalm* 149:2, 3).

King David's Dance

David danced a leaping dance of ecstasy before the Ark of God: 'David, wearing
a linen ephod (a hip-length tunic), danced before the Lord with all his
might...leaping and dancing before the Lord' (2 *Samuel* 6:14–16). This is dance
before it developed into a religious rite: here it is a rhythmic release of energy,
an ecstatic act. Only gradually was dance transformed from spontaneous movement to a fixed pattern of steps, gestures and poses, but through both forms, the
dancer aspired to approach God. The body became an instrument for transcendent power, and this power was encountered directly in the dance. The fourth
century Green theologian Gregory Nazianzen wrote: 'Dance the dance of David
before the ark of the covenant, for I believe that such a dance holds the mystery
of walking in the sight of God (Wosien 1974, p.29).

Ancient Israelites indicated the esteem in which they held dance by describing their hero, King David, dancing for God. Christians, too, held dance in great
respect, and even popes created dances, as David did before them. When Pope
Urban IV inaugurated the feast of Corpus Christi in 1264, he declared: 'Let faith
pray, hope sing, and charity dance for joy'. He established a dance before the
altar of Seville cathedral which is still danced at Easter by its choristers, in spite
of many efforts to abolish it (Haynes 1990, p.7). It is accompanied by singing
and castanets.

Seizure and Ecstasy

As well as channelling divine power, dance puts us in touch with our inner
being. In dance, we transcend fragmentation, and feel one both with ourselves
and with the external world. In the experience of seizure and rapture, a person
becomes related to the universe, to the whole of life. Old Testament prophets
encountered God in this way. Samuel told Saul: 'You will go to Gibeah... As you
approach the town, you will meet a procession of prophets coming down from
the high place with lyres, tambourines, flutes and harps being played before
them, and they will be prophesying. The Spirit of the Lord will seize you, and
you will go into an ecstasy with them, and be changed into a different person'
(1 *Samuel* 10:5, 6). Saul was drawn into their group consciousness; the group's
ritual dance and music stimulated their awareness of God.

In dance we enter sacred time, which is timeless, eternal; and we enter into
harmony with all creation. We thus transcend the created world and enter
paradise. St. Luke describes how John the Baptist danced for joy in his mother
Elizabeth's womb. He danced because he encountered Jesus, the new ark of the
covenant, in the womb of Mary. Elizabeth says to Mary: 'The moment your
greeting reached my ears, the child in my womb leaped for joy' (*Luke* 1:44). John

leapt for joy as, centuries before, David leapt for joy before the old ark of the covenant.

Animal Rituals

Ancient peoples learnt to dance from watching animals and birds, imitating their sounds and movements in an attempt to capture the life and power within them. Cranes, in their mating dance, raise their wings, lift their feet, sink their heads into their breasts and lift them again, while shuffling round in a circle. They accompany their movements with irregular, rhythmic sounds, part song, part cry. In Zaïre, girls of the Watussi tribe perform the dance of the crowned cranes (Wosien 1974).

Julian Huxley observed the pair-bonding rituals of birds. He noted that among egrets, grebes and herons, 'when a pair was re-united after one partner had come back from fishing, there was great vocal excitement, with bobbing of heads and fluttering of wings', until 'the returning bird went off to gather twigs which he or she ceremonially offered to its mate, who then built them into the nest', accepting the token of renewed relationship, and weaving it into their common home. For these birds, nestbuilding is both a task and a dance. Huxley noted that for animals, ritual behaviour has several functions: to trigger off sexual, aggressive or flight reactions, or to strengthen pair-bonding (Huxley 1973, p.228). Such animal rituals are the origins of human mating rituals (wedding dances), aggressive rituals (war dances) and of our communal dances of celebration.

Animals have a variety of courtship rituals, individual and collective. One type involves bringing something to eat: a bird may offer a worm, as we may offer a box of chocolates to a friend, or Israelites offered grain or a kid or some pigeons to God. Another courtship ritual is a stylised formal dance, like the mating dance of great crested cranes, the circles which rutting stags trace in the woods, or the squeaking, scuttering mating dance of the hedgehog, which trots round its partner in diminishing circles until they finally mate, face to face (Haynes 1990, p.7). Tortoises perform a rather slow mating dance, in which one partner follows behind its mate, periodically clonking the tail end of its shell. Dogs ritualise their violence in play, as they channel aggression into mock fighting.

Early peoples observed animals closely, since they depended on them for food, clothing, tools and weapons. People saw animals as their ancestors, admiring in animals the qualities they lacked, such as the bear's strength and the swiftness of birds. In the soft clay of the Ice Age Tuc d'Audubert cave in France, Herbert Kühn found footprints that led around painted animal figures, where people had danced. Kühn wrote: 'Only heel prints can be seen; the dancers had moved like bison. They had danced a bison dance for the fertility and increase of the animals, and for their slaughter' (Jaffé 1964, pp.235–237). In temple courts in Bali, men gather at night round a burning torch to celebrate the monkey-trance dance, or Ketjak. It is a dance of exorcism based on a Hindu myth, in which the sounds and movements aim to drive away evil. At the climax of the dance, the chorus crouch at the feet of their leader and gather in two semicircles facing each other. With powerful cries and wild gestures they drive away the demons of night, and then fall back into silence.

American Indians in the southwestern deserts perform harvest dances in which the women carry green branches and wear rainbow headdresses to ask for rain for the crops. They also perform deer dances in the winter, butterfly

23. **Eagle dancer in the American Southwest.** *He imitates the eagle's majestic power. (From a photograph)*

dances in which the children are prominent, buffalo dances for a successful hunt, and eagle dances. For Indians living in the deserts of the southwest and in Mexico, the blazing sun is their most immediate image of divine power, and the eagle is seen as the sun's child. The Papago Indians of the southwest chant this song as they ask to receive the eagle's strength:

> The sun's rays
> lie along my wings
> and stretch beyond their tips. (Astrov 1962, p.16)

The Cora Indians of Mexico perform a magnificent eagle chant, a portion of which runs:

> Under the sky the eagle, there he abides,
> there far above us.
> Beautiful he appears.
> In his talons he holds the world.
> A grey garment he wears,
> a beautiful living-moist garment of clouds.
> Bright-eyed he looks down upon his world.
> Towards the west his eyes are turned.
> Bright-eyed he looks down upon the waters of life.
> His countenance radiates calamity.
> Magnificent in his eye, the sun! (Astrov 1962, p.323).

Processional Dance

Dance imitates; it aims to achieve identity with the thing observed and danced out. Dance re-creates all kinds of occurrences from life in rhythmic play. Early rituals represent divine power experienced in creation: the power of the soaring eagle, or the gentle growth of the crops during rain. Later peoples such as the ancient Babylonians and Israelites humanised God, and through their rituals represented his act of creation and his presence among us. Ancient Babylonians danced the mystery of creation from chaos, which they symbolically represented as a battle, and re-enacted at the start of each year. By doing so, the dancer was put in touch with that primal event, and also enabled to continue it. The Israelites danced their salvation history in triumphal processional dances.

Psalm 68 describes a ritual of this kind. It is a processional liturgy re-enacting God's triumphant march from Mount Sinai in the wilderness (under Moses) to Mount Sion (under David). The ark of God's presence accompanies God's people on their triumphant journey. The start of the procession recalls the beginning of God's march with his ragged army of runaway slaves:

> May God arise, may his foes be scattered;
> may his foes flee before him (*Psalm* 68:1).

Eventually, the procession reaches the sanctuary:

> Your procession has come into view, O God,
> the procession of my God and king into the sanctuary.
> In front are the singers, after them the musicians;
> with them are the maidens playing tambourines (*Psalm* 68:24, 25).

St. Paul quotes verses from this psalm to imply that Christ ascending into the heavens continues the joyful procession:

> The Lord has come from Sinai into his sanctuary.
> When you ascended on high, you led captives in your train,
> you received gifts from men (*Psalm* 68:17, 18 = *Ephesians* 4:8–13).

Another ritual procession is described in Psalm 118. Perhaps used at the feast of Tabernacles, it again celebrates victory and deliverance by God:

> Shouts of joy and victory resound in the tents of the righteous:
> 'The Lord's right hand has done mighty things!...
> Open for me the gates of righteousness;
> I will enter and give thanks to the Lord...'
> With branches in hand, join in the festal procession
> up to the horns of the altar (*Psalm* 118:15, 19, 27).

The crowds who greeted Jesus on his triumphal entry into Jerusalem joined in the festal procession with branches in hand, chanting words from this psalm: 'Blessed is he who comes in the name of the Lord' (*Psalm* 118:26), thus making the psalm their own, and receiving life through doing so.

Dance as a Sacrament

A festal procession is a sacred dance; and dance is a symbol or sacrament, making real what it signifies, both for the dancer and for the world. Creation constantly needs renewal, and ritual releases life into the world, to renew it. Catholics leave Mass feeling renewed and knowing that, on some level, the celebration has brought new life and harmony to their world. Participants at Mass are brought in touch with primordial reality, thus releasing emotional tension, giving birth to new hope and receiving life. All true ritual effects this; it is a symbolic representation of ultimate reality.

Since ritual is a representation of a primordial event, it is danced carefully, with great attention to detail. The sounds and movements of a ritual belonging to a race or tribe will continue for thousands of years without substantial changes. Thirty years ago, the Second Vatican Council altered the ritual of the Mass, and this aroused fearful reactions too deep for words in the hearts of many Catholics. As the sacred dance movements are repeated, dancers relive experiences related to their origin, and so enter the divine world, to be made a little more divine. Ritual dance has no audience: it involves all present, and is addressed to God. When ritual dance is separated from worship, it is marginalised into folk dances and games. Anthropologists then have the detective task of reconstructing the original ritual. An example of an ancient sacred dance surviving in folk custom is that performed round the maypole. This was originally a dance round the tree of life, the world axis linking heaven and earth.

At most times, and for most peoples, dance has been a central concern of their lives. All the arts later emerged from danced ritual: mask-making, sacred vestments, the construction of sacred spaces in which to enact ritual, and pictorial representations of holy ceremonies. Dance takes a significant fragment of human life, repeats it and celebrates it, establishing a relationship with it. In this way we can solidify our fleeting life and give it support. It gives us a frame of reference, and enables us to leap over the boundary of consciousness.

Human Acts are Holy Acts

Early peoples experienced human life as holy; almost all human activities were considered to be sacred. Christian sacraments began as basic human activities which were perceived to be holy: a bath, a meal, an embrace, rubbing with fragrant oil, and these actions took place within the family atmosphere of the house church. Baptism in the first Christian centuries was a procession with oil lamps to a pool or to the family baths, where candidates were rubbed all over with oil, immersed and dressed in new clothes (Guzie 1981, p.130). Christians tend to think that their founder, Jesus, invented such rituals, but they predate Christianity and are found in many cultures. Hindus wash in holy waters, offer rice and flowers, and worship by travelling on pilgrimage to shrines. Washing, walking and offering rice are at once ordinary actions and holy ones.

Archaic peoples perceived divine power at work in animals, who gave them food so they could live. Later peoples thought of God in human form. When people became sufficiently familiar with their gods to name them and ascribe functions to them, they created myths. For an individual to become an adult member of his or her community, he or she needed to know its myths, take part in its rituals and understand its symbols. These were the ways in which the community encountered the sacred. We require the same of someone joining a Church today: he or she must know its myths, its sacred stories, take part in its rituals, and understand its symbols.

Death Rituals

The mystery of death is the greatest challenge to the human mind, so the earliest ceremonies we know are those for the dead. Burial was extremely important to ancient peoples. Abraham purchased his first piece of the promised land from the Canaanites as a burial plot for his wife, Sarah (*Genesis* 23:19). To this day, those with little or no belief in God know the deep importance of a funeral. The loved one may be buried in the ground, or the ashes scattered, but somehow, those left alive must help the dead towards their rebirth.

A ritual death-dance normally portrays the battle of the dead person with the demons of darkness, and his or her victory over them. The dance uses strong rhythms, loud music and wailing mourners. When Jairus's daughter died, Jesus saw the people 'crying and wailing loudly'. Jesus told them that these death laments were inappropriate, since the child was not permanently dead: 'He went in and said to them, "Why all this commotion and wailing? The child is not dead but asleep"' (*Mark* 5:38, 39). Often dancers encircle the bier or funeral pyre and perform a chain dance with interlinked arms, to protect the dead person from the power of darkness and to call on the power of life. At a Catholic funeral, the priest sprinkles the coffin with holy water, living water, and encircles it as he offers incense to God.

24. *A ritual funeral dance performed by women linking hands, Roman, 5th century B.C.* *(Drawing by Steven Nemethy, based on a tomb painting from Ruvo in the National Archeological Museum, Naples)*

Christianity has separated out evil powers (devils) from good powers (angels), but in less complex cultures, powers of light and darkness are both experienced as holy. Terrible demons represent the dark, destructive aspect of creation. They wear masks and dance in blazing flames, alive in the transforming fire. In the ecstasy of the dance, fear is transformed into rapture, and behind the terrifying mask of the demon, a beneficent guide is discovered (Wosien 1974, p.15). King Nebuchadnezzar threw Daniel's three friends into a blazing furnace, where they were not destroyed, but met an angel of God: Nebuchadnezzar said, 'Look! I see four men walking around in the fire, unbound and unharmed, and the fourth looks like a son of the gods' (*Daniel* 3:25). Fire and heat symbolise transformation.

Wedding and War Dances

Marriage rituals are important in many cultures, including our own. They symbolise the life-giving union of heaven and earth. The joining of the man and woman ensures fertility and long life. In many ceremonies, the man and woman are dressed in the robes of king and queen and wear ritual crowns (as at Orthodox weddings) as a symbol of their union. Our marriage dance is a solemn procession of bride and groom down the centre aisle of the church to the altar steps. The couple wear ceremonial clothes; music plays; flowers are carried and attendants follow them.

Sacred dances took place at all major events and seasons: birth, puberty, marriage, battle, victory and death. Also at hunt, seedtime and harvest, as well as at sudden frightening events which broke upon the community. In early dance, the human body was the sound-producing instrument, through stamping feet, clapping hands and slapping of thighs. The sexes were normally segregated, since they had different roles. Men danced sun, war and most animal-spirit dances, and dances for rain and healing. Women danced fertility, rain and harvest dances, and birth and mourning rituals. The oldest dances are circular and choral; line dances gradually replaced them. At first the dancer sang his accompaniment; later, an instrument replaced the voice (Wosien 1974, pp.16, 17).

Early peoples fought to preserve the sacred territory of their god; the Old Testament is one long chronicle of such battles. Each tribe went to war to reinstate the original order of creation (from which grew the Islamic concept of a holy war), and so a war dance concerns the struggle of good against evil. Joshua and the Israelite army performed a war dance when they encircled Jericho with a sacred procession, carrying the ark of the covenant, with seven priests blowing ramshorn trumpets, and warriors shouting a war cry. To encircle a space is to claim it for God, and through their holy circling, God gave them the city (*Joshua* 6). In ancient Greece, commanders in battle were called 'principal dancers', and Socrates wrote: 'the men who dance best are the best warriors' (Wosien 1974, p.102).

Birth into Heavenly Life

Ritual intensifies experience until catharsis is achieved. Christians use a variety of techniques to focus awareness and open the participant to the transcendent. Charismatics sing songs as they prepare together to receive the Spirit of God. Worshippers before Mass may kneel in silence to recollect (gather together) themselves; until recently they would recite 'prayers before Mass'. In the early Church, catechumens prepared to experience the mystery of Easter by fasting and by others praying for them. The forty days of Lent are traditionally a time of prayer and fasting through which the whole Christian community prepares to celebrate the mystery of Christ's resurrection at Easter.

25. *Turkish harvest dance performed at a*
    wedding, in which the whole community
    asks that the fruitful union of the couple
    may be mirrored by the fruitfulness of the
    fields.1. Before the dance, women fill gourds
    with water to mime rain watering the cornseed.
    Photograph: Margaret Rees

26. *Turkish harvest dance performed at a*
    wedding. 2. The bridegroom demonstrates
    his prowess. *Photograph: Margaret Rees*

27. *Turkish harvest dance performed at a wedding. 3. Women dance with water, while men*
    dance with sickles as they mime the harvest. Photograph: Margaret Rees

The Greek and Roman mystery cults carried abandonment to the transcendent to extreme limits. In the cult of the god Dionysus, or Bacchus, wine was used to free the novice to abandon himself to his instincts and experience erotic fulfilment, the creative power of the god. This fulfilment was symbolised by the marriage of Dionysus to Ariadne. Brides were also initiated into this cult: a villa in Pompeii belonging to a priestess of the cult appears to portray in murals the stages of such a ceremony. In the paintings, a novice listens to the sacred reading, makes an offering of bread, and has water poured over her hands. She drinks wine, and venerates sacred objects. She is then scourged, before dancing in ecstasy, accompanying herself with handbells.

In sacred dance, ritual transformation enables spiritual rebirth. Physical birth produces physical people; the living spirit is brought into being by a second birth. As Jesus explains to Nicodemus: 'Unless a man is born from above, he cannot see the kingdom of God... What is born of the flesh is flesh; what is born of the Spirit is spirit' (*John* 3:3–6). In the ecstasy of sacred dance, the participant dies to self and is transformed into God for a time.

28. *Jewish men dancing in prayer, led by a shawm-player.* (From a print by Mogal, Israel)

The Body as a Sacred Vessel

Early peoples considered the physical body to be sacred. Food, drink, breathing and sex were sacred channels through which divine power could enter us. To convey the holiness of the body, many cultures decorate the body, to show that it is transformed; it is an ornamented vessel in which God dwells. St. Paul explains that we contain the divine treasure in earthen vessels (2 *Corinthians* 4:7). He also writes that we are temples of God's Spirit: 'Do you not know that your body is a temple of the Holy Spirit who is in you, whom you have received from God?... Therefore honour God with your body' (1 *Corinthians* 3:16; 6:19). The head was often masked or covered, as the seat of divine power. Women's veils in marriage and in religious life from St. Paul's time to this day indicate this respect for the divinity. When contemporary nuns take off the veil, people can respond with quite irrational anger at this loss of respect for the deity within.

Ritual expresses our relationship with God; it is universal and timeless, because it is concerned with offering praise to God, or at the very least, with affirming life as it is. The language of ritual gesture is found everywhere; its form and style is prescribed in each culture. Ritual keeps a group and its individual members in touch with the divine. It was only late in history that the spoken word replaced movement as the means of worship. Thirty years ago, the Second Vatican Council tried to restore the balance by encouraging us to worship God with 'actions, gestures and bodily attitudes' (*Constitution on the Sacred Liturgy* 1966, para. 30). The gestures of the Mass are as powerful as its words. As the priest enters, we rise to begin something memorable. Next we make the sign of the cross, covering our bodies with the passion of Jesus. We sit, in receptive posture, to receive the word of God. We stand in reverence for the gospel. We process to the altar to bring our offerings and to receive communion. During the central portion of the Mass, we stand in reverence or kneel in awe. To kneel is to reduce ourselves to half our height. We may pray the Our Father with outstretched hands, an ancient posture of prayer. We might still strike our breasts as we say 'Lord, I am not worthy'. We embrace each other in whatever way is natural at the greeting of peace.

Sacred Space

A sacred building provides a framework for worship, and transforms chaos into cosmos. A square domed temple, church or mosque represents the earth (which was thought to be square) crowned by the dome of the heavens. In this building, heaven meets earth. The pantheon in Rome, first a temple then a church, is a domed circular building, a place for heavenly encounter, with a central opening to the sky. Early peoples chose to live in a space opening upwards so that they could communicate ritually with the transcendent world. They needed to live at the heart of the real, at the centre of the world, where they could be closest to the divine. Countries and cities, palaces and temples, tents and huts each had a sacred centre. The sky was conceived as a vast tent supported by a central pillar, and the tent pole of a nomad's tent resembles this world pillar, and may be named after it (*Eliade* 1957, pp.42–53). It is a ladder to heaven, like Jacob's ladder, on which he saw the angels of God ascend and descend (*Genesis* 28:10).

A sacred way leads up to a sacred building. At Delphi and other Greek shrines, market stalls at the entrance to the sacred way enabled worshippers to purchase offerings. This was necessary because sacrifice was part of worship, as it was in Jerusalem where Jesus was angered by the hustling at the temple gates, and overturned the market stalls in defence of the temple's holiness (*Matthew* 21:12–14). At Delphi, the worshipper climbed the Sacred Way, passing treasuries, the gifts of wealthy cities, until he reached the great temple at its summit. Only the pure could walk the Sacred Way, so worshippers camped beside a sacred spring until they were ready for the ascent. The prophet Isaiah describes God's Sacred Way:

> They will see the glory of the Lord, the splendour of our God...
> And a highway will be there;
> it will be called the Sacred Way.
> The unclean will not journey on it (*Isaiah* 35:2, 8).

The sacred precinct was closed by gates, to protect the cosmic holy space from the chaos beyond. To enter the gates was to put on holiness. In Psalm 118 the worshipper chants:

> Open for me the gates of holiness;
> I will enter and give thanks to the Lord (*Psalm* 118:19).

St. Paul caused a riot in Jerusalem when Jewish worshippers thought he had brought a gentile into the sacred temple. At this time, gentiles were not allowed beyond the Court of the Gentiles, which was marked off from the temple by a stone balustrade with slabs inscribed in Latin and Greek warning foreigners of the death penalty if they trespassed. The Jews shut the temple gates to defend the holiness within: 'The whole city was aroused, and the people came running from all directions. Seizing Paul, they dragged him from the temple, and immediately the gates were shut' (*Acts* 21:27–30). They tried to kill Paul for profaning the holy place.

Journey through Life's Maze

Pilgrimages are still made along sacred paths, round holy mountains and to holy shrines. Irish Catholics climb Croagh Patrick; other pilgrims journey to the cave at Lourdes in the Pyrenees, a shrine of Our Lady, or to the cave of the Nativity of Jesus in Bethlehem. Pilgrimage is the oldest of religious activities; it has been practised in every culture since megalithic times. The sanctuary may lie under the earth (saints are often buried in a church's crypt), or it may occupy a mountain peak. Catholics walk the Way of the Cross in procession, pausing fouteen times to remember the last actions of Jesus, often winding up a hill as they do so. Their outward act of encircling helps an inner reorientation towards the divine.

The cosmic significance of pilgrimage for Hindus is beautifully described by Michael Barnes: 'The temple is the centre of the universe; the pilgrim is following the gift of life back to its source. When pilgrims enter the temple, they are returning to the cosmic harmony from which they came. Pilgrimage, that simplest of all human liturgies, represents the human return to God' (Barnes 1991, p.38). Pilgrimage is one of the most popular forms of worship for Hindus today.

Outside prehistoric cave sanctuaries a maze may be traced, to enable dancers to enact a spirit's wandering before it enters new life. The Cretan story of Theseus wandering in the labyrinth was enacted in ritual dance. Theseus came to represent Christ descending to the underworld, overcoming Satan (the minotaur), and emerging with the people he had saved. From the eleventh century, labyrinths are found in many European churches, inlaid in the floor of the nave. In Auxerre cathedral, the ball dance was performed on the labyrinth on Easter day to the music of the Easter sequence 'Victimae paschali laudes'. The dean and canons solemnly threw and caught a ball, which represented Christ, the risen Easter sun, and afterwards shared a meal (Rahner (ii) 1963, p.85).

The Dance of Jesus

The Apocryphal Acts of St. John describe a Dance of Jesus, which was understood as an initiation ritual in the fourth century. It was a danced hymn of praise, through which the dancers shared the suffering and rising of Christ. In the dance Christ, the leader, stood in the centre, and dancers representing the twelve apostles moved round him in a circle:

> He gathered all of us together and said:
> 'Before I am delivered up to them,
> let us sing a hymn to the Father,
> and so go forth to that which lies before us.'
> He bade us therefore make, as it were, a ring,
> holding one another's hands,
> and himself standing in the centre, he said:
> 'Answer Amen to me'
> He began then to sing a hymn and to say:
> 'Glory be to you, Father!'
> And we, going about in a ring, answered him: 'Amen'
> (Wosien 1974, p.28).

St. Ambrose, fourth century bishop of Milan, describes how we each have the right to join in the circle dance of creation: 'Just as he who dances with his body, rushing through the rotating movements of the limbs, acquires a right to share in the round dance, in the same way, he who dances the spiritual dance, always moving in the ecstasy of faith, acquires a right to dance in the ring of all creation'.

To commemorate the festivals of virgin saints, Ambrose wrote a hymn describing how these women follow their bridegroom Christ in the heavenly dance:

> You walk among lilies
> Surrounded by choirs of virgins,
> Bridegroom fair in your glory.
> Wherever you go,
> Virgins follow in your train,
> Singing (*Liber Usialis* 1947, p.1021).

The Jewish Talmud, or commentary on the scriptures, describes dancing as the chief function of the angels. Angels were thought of by Christians as present at Mass, adoring their Lord, and medieval art often portrays them singing and dancing. Botticelli (sixteenth century) paints them performing a joyful round dance over the stable at the birth of Christ. They carry olive branches, bringing peace to the world, and toss their coronets around. Fra Angelico (fifteenth century) portrays angels inviting saints into the round dance of heaven, in a painting of paradise. The early theologians invited the faithful to join the angels. St. Basil, fourth century bishop of Caesaria asked: 'Could there be anything more blessed than to imitate on earth the ring dance of the angels, and at dawn to raise our voices in prayer, and by hymns and songs to glorify the rising Creator?' (Wosien 1974, p.29).

29. *Jewish men dancing with the scroll of the Law. (From a print by N. Cohen, Israel)*

30. *The Mystic Nativity*, by *Sandro Botticelli (c.1445–1510).*
Twelve angels perform a circle dance above the stable, clasping hands and holding palms and crowns. Three more angels sing an accompaniment. Their sacred dance proclaims that heaven is wedded to earth at this moment. (Courtesy of the National Gallery, London.

Carols

In medieval times, the simplest sacred dance was the carol. The word comes from the Green 'choraulein' (*choros* = dance; *aulein* = to play the flute). It was a circle dance accompanied by singing, normally in triple time, and often with verses (sung by the leader) and a chorus. The early Franciscans linked carols with Christmas, and carols quickly spread to Spain and France, and then to England and Germany, where Dominican preachers and theologians such as Eckhardt, Tauler and Suso wrote carols. There were various types, such as lullabies or shepherds' carols. The Coventry carol 'Lully thou little tiny child' is a lament for the Holy Innocents written for one of the miracle plays. The Boar's Head carol is an early feasting carol, sung in a great hall (Dearmer, Vaughan Williams and Shaw 1928, no.19, p.37).

A carol from a miracle play describes the life of Jesus as a dance which we, his true love, are invited to join:

>Tomorrow shall be my dancing day:
>I would my true love did so chance
>To see the legend of my play,
>To call my true love to the dance.
>Sing, oh! my love, oh! my love, my love;
>This have I done for my true love.
>
>In a manger laid and wrapp'd I was
>So very poor, this was my chance,
>Betwixt an ox and a silly poor ass,
>To call my true love to my dance.
>Sing, oh! my love, oh! my love, my love;
>This have I done for my true love.

The carol continues through the life and death of Jesus, until we reach 'the general dance' of heaven with him:

>Then up to heaven I did ascend,
>Where now I dwell in sure substance,
>On the right hand of God, that man
>May come unto the general dance.
>   (Dearmer, Vaughan Williams and Shaw 1928, no.71, pp.154–155).

The Heavenly Circle Dance

The author of the book of *Revelation* provides a magnificent picture of the sacred dance of heaven, in which all of creation encircles God's throne, falling down in worship and singing praise: 'I saw a Lamb looking as if it had been slain, standing in the centre of the throne, encircled by the four living creatures and the elders... They lay down their crowns before the throne... The 24 elders fell down before the Lamb. Each one had a harp (to accompany their song) and they were holding golden bowls full of incense, which are the prayers of the saints.

And they sang a new song... Then I looked and heard the voice of many angels, numbering thousands upon thousands... They encircled the throne and the elders. In a loud voice they sang: "Worthy is the Lamb who was slain..." Then I heard every creature in heaven and on earth and under the earth and on the sea, and all that is in them, singing:

> "To him who sits on the throne and to the Lamb be praise and honour and glory and power for ever and ever!"

The four living creatures said "Amen", and the elders fell down and worshipped' (*Revelation* 4:5).

This is perhaps a more active heaven than some of us might like; eternal rest may sound more attractive. But the concepts the author of *Revelation* wished to convey are harmony, movement and joy. It is not too difficult now to find a group who meet for circle dancing; they exist in most towns. Anyone who takes the time to join them will know, however fleetingly, the harmony and communion which the author of *Revelation* describes.

Symbol and Integration

What inner need urges us to create symbols? Our search for integration compels us to do so. We use symbols to reach beyond our everyday experience in order to find deeper meaning. Symbols address our basic needs and fears, especially our fear of death, and so through symbols we make sense of our journey between birth and death. Symbols give us markers, goals, and a rough plan of our journey. They also provide a divine context for our journey, connecting us with the transcendent at every point along the way.

What can we do with symbols? As a people, we are not fully at home with symbol-making. We are a functional people, but symbols can never be functional. Symbols point to the divine, and God is not a functional being. If we ask, 'How can we use God?' or 'What can we do with God?', we are asking the wrong kind of question. So too, symbols are not functional; they speak of a different order of being. We cannot command symbols to 'work' for us: they are too big for that. The most we can do is open ourselves to their power.

Throughout the ages, people have used symbols for healing and personal integration, and this has normally taken place in the context of ritual. Ritual is a holy, symbolic action: we walk across the bridge of ritual into the world of the transcendent. A ritual is a symbolic journey towards wholeness. Much of this book has been concerned with the elements that make up ritual: movement and gesture, chanting and natural symbols. In ritual we take with us such symbols as bread, water and fire, and use them as a language with which to contact God.

We have also considered the phenomenon of holy leadership. In many rituals, the worshippers identify with their leader, who has become a symbol for them. Their leader is now a hero who has successfully travelled the journey into the transcendent otherworld. We may be unwilling to admit our need to identify with a leader, but we all tend to do so. In worship, our leader is taken out of himself by us: we turn him into a symbol, with whom we enter communion.

Worship is a group phenomenon: it is something we do in a group. The first thing a group normally does is to look for a leader. In this way the Israelites found Moses, their intercessor with God. Later legends of Moses describe him as a hero whose origins were uncertain, who was adopted by the great pharaoh and who received a mystical call from God. Moses was also a guilt-laden murderer who ran away from his people and so established himself outside their order of experience. He then returned to his people and took them into liberation. The existence of the Israelites as a free people began when they identified with their leader, Moses (van der Kleij 1991).

When worshippers identify with a leader, they may imitate their hero. Spanish Christian *penitentes* imitate the suffering of Jesus by scourging themselves, while some Filipinos nail themselves to a cross on Good Friday to imitate their leader. The symbols they choose, however, distort the truth. Spanish penitents may torture themselves to imitate their leader, Jesus, whom they lovingly believe was tortured to atone for their sins, but a truer Christian tradition celebrates Jesus as a liberator and bringer of peace.

Worship, Violence and Communion

What is the purpose of worship? Perhaps a major function of worship is to contain group violence: we take our communal violence and act it out ritually. When a pack of dogs fight in play, they contain their aggressive energy through doing so. Instead of killing each other, they act out their need for dominance in play. This can be seen as one of the origins of liturgy. The Old Testament records constant efforts to cope with the violence of the group. Once a year the Jews symbolically loaded their violence onto a scapegoat and sent it out into the desert to rid the group of the violence lurking below the surface of the community (*Leviticus* 16:20–22) (van der Kleij 1991).

At Mass, Christians symbolically load their violence onto Jesus, the Lamb of God, who takes the violence and its perpetrators and offers them to God. Participants pray: 'Lamb of God, you take away the sins of the world. Grant us peace'. In this way, ritual contains our violence, and so transforms it. Such symbols as the scapegoat and the Lamb of God cause transformation; as we enter into symbols, our violence is transformed into communion. Only symbols can transform the death of Good Friday into the resurrection of Easter for us. Symbols refashion us, and that is why we need them.

Our Earliest Liturgy: A Thank You

I will end by describing the earliest recorded ancient Jewish liturgy. It is an act of thanksgiving, which is carried out in a simpler form today at each harvest festival. In this ceremony, repeated by generations of ancient Jews, the participant put his fruit and vegetables into a basket, came before the priest and claimed his symbolic origin by declaring: 'My father was a wandering Aramean. He went down into Egypt to find refuge there'. The participant described how, symbolically, he himself was rescued from Egyptian slavery by God and brought to a land flowing with milk and honey. He concluded: 'Here, then, I bring the first fruits of the produce of the soil that you, Lord, have given me' (*Deuteronomy* 26:1–11).

This declaration is both our earliest statement of belief (or creed) and our first liturgy. The Hebrew farmers who created it may have copied the ceremonies of tribes living around them for, since famine was a matter of life and death, tribal farmers would probably bring their first fruits as offerings to please their gods or to bargain with them. However the ancient Israelite, according to this text, handed over his basket to the priest, not to placate the gods, but to acknowledge that God had given him such fertile land. He brought his basket of figs and water melons, or of corn and wine, in a powerful symbolic act of thanks.

As Christians give thanks in their Eucharist today, the Israelite farmer came to meet and thank his gracious God. As he gave thanks in this simple ritual, he experienced the magnificent presence of God who comes to meet us as we go to meet Him. He expressed his awe by falling on his face and kissing the ground in worship, in a spontaneous ritual gesture (*Deuteronomy* 26:10). The ceremony these farmers enacted appears to be a spring festival of the kind which Moses wanted to take his people into the desert to celebrate. This grew into the Jewish Passover meal, in which thanksgiving for their land and for their history are interwoven. It is likely that the Last Supper of Jesus was a Passover meal, into which Jesus inserted his own life-giving story.

The Jewish farmer's ritual ended on a concrete note, as he and his family feasted on the good things he had brought, for his symbols belonged to real life as well as to the transcendent world. He was also asked to share his food with the priest and the needy stranger (*Deuteronomy* 26:11), for symbols remain stillborn if they are not brought into the real world of other people. And so these farmers used symbols to give life to themselves and to their world. We can do the same.

Appendix

It can be of value to play with symbols ourselves, so that we make them our own, and come to feel more deeply the connections between ourselves and the universe in which we live. Here are some suggestions about how to do so, which teachers may also find useful for students.

Chapter 2. Corn, The Bread of Life

1. Find a cornfield at any season of the year. Sit at its edge, and draw what you see.

2. Choose a recipe, and bake bread. While it is still warm, eat it and share it.

3. Go to a church, not of your denomination. Attend a communion service there.

Chapter 3. Water and Blood; The Ark of Safety

1. Spend an afternoon walking along a river bank or seashore. Be attentive to the life at the water's edge.

2. Choose a large sheet of paper, and draw a coloured picture of the river of your life, starting at the spring of your birth.

3. Do some brisk exercise, then relax and feel your pulse beat for five minutes. As you do so, picture the blood flowing through different parts of your body.

Chapter 4. The Snake in Paradise Lost and Regained

1. Go to a market and buy a toy snake, the bigger and brighter, the better. Spend some time playing with your snake.

2. Choose an animal and become it for fifteen minutes. How does it feel?

3. Draw a monster; then draw a paradise. Don't make it a boring one!

Chapter 5. The Tree of Life and the Tree of the Cross

1. On a walk, find an old tree and take a while to rest, upright, against its trunk, sensing its support.

2. Draw yourself as a tree.

3. Write a story in the life of your tree.

Chapter 6. Sun and Moon; Fire and Light

1. Spend a month following the moon through its phases.

2. Sit in a candlelit room for a while and relax. Experience the new atmosphere.

3. Light a fire, in or out of doors, and watch the flames dance.

Chapter 7. Symbols of Jesus and Mary in Art

1. Choose a pre–seventeenth century religious painting. Decide why you like it.

2. Identify symbols in the painting.

3. Using the painting as a focus, talk to God, however you experience him/her/it.

Chapter 8. Priest and Shaman: Holy Leaders

1. Think of someone who has been a spiritual leader for you. List three ways they have shown God to you.

2. Invent a religion. Write its rules; draw a picture of its leader.

3. List three ways in which you are a holy leader, e.g. in your family.

Chapter 9. Chant and Incantation: Sacred Song

1. What music is most powerful for you? Why?

2. What music most soothes or heals you? Why?

3. Make up a simple prayer and give it a tune. Quietly sing it during the course of a whole day.

Chapter 10. Ritual: the Dance of Heaven and Earth

1. Think of a religious service which affected you, e.g. a wedding or a funeral. Write a sentence describing what was for you the most powerful moment in the service.

2. You have invented a new Church. Think up a ceremony for a new member to join your church. Write it down. You can confer a symbol on the new member, e.g. a key, an apple, a drink.

3. Work out a farewell ceremony for a married couple about to separate. Write it down.

Bibliography

Arbeau, T. (1967) *Orchesography*. M. Stewart Evans (trans.). New York: Dover Publications.

Armstrong, R. and Brady, I. (trans.)(1982) *Francis and Clare. The Complete Works*. London: Society for Promotion of Christian Knowledge.

Astrov, M. (1962) *American Indian Prose and Poetry: an Anthology*. New York: Capricorn Books.

Athanasius, *Vita S. Antonii* (1950). In Migne, J.P. '*Patrologiae cursus completus. Series graeco-latina*' no. 26, columns 835–976. R. Meyer (trans.) *Ancient Christian Writers* vol. 10. London: Longmans, Green & Co.

Atkinson, C. (1983) *Mystic and Pilgrim: the Book and World of Margery Kempe*. Ithaca, New York: Cornell University Press.

Baring-Gould, S. (1897) *The Lives of the Saints*. London: John Nimmo.

Barnes, M. (1991) *God East and West*. London: S.P.C.K.

Briand, J. (1982) *The Judeo-Christian Church of Nazareth*. Jerusalem: Franciscan Printing Press.

Brown, J.E. (1985) 'North American Religions'. In J. Hinnells (ed.) *A Handbook of Living Religions*. London: Penguin.

Buber, M. (1947) *Tales of the Hasidim: the Early Masters*. New York: Schocken Books.

Bunyan, J. (1951) *The Pilgrim's Progress*. R. Warner (ed.). London: News of the World.

Butler-Bowden, W. (ed)(1936) *The Book of Margery Kempe*. Oxford University Press.

Carmichael, A. (1900) *Carmina Gadelica, Hymns and Incantations with illustrative notes of words, rites and customs dying and obsolete: orally collected in the Highlands and Islands of Scotland*. Edinburgh: Scottish Academic Press.

Carter, S. (1963) *Lord of the Dance*. London: Stainer and Bell.

Catherine of Siena, St. (1905) 'Letter to Raymond of Capua'. In V. Scudder (trans.) *St. Catherine as seen in her Letters*. London: Dent.

Catherine of Siena, St. (1925) 'Treatise on Prayer' In A. Thorold (ed) *The Dialogue of the Seraphic Virgin, Catherine of Siena*. London: Burns, Oates and Washbourne.

Christian, R. (1987) *Well-dressing in Derbyshire*. Derby: Derbyshire Countryside Ltd.

Cirlot, J.E. (1962) *A Dictionary of Symbols*, transl. J. Sage. New York: Philosophical Library.

Constitution on the Sacred Liturgy (1966). In W. Abbot (ed.) *Documents of Vatican II*. London: Geoffrey Chapman.

Cronyn, G. (1918) *The Path of the Rainbow*. New York: Boni and Liveright.

Crum, J.M.C. (1977) 'Now the Green Blade Riseth', hymn S3 in *The Complete Celebration Hymnal*. Great Wakering, Essex: Mayhew McCrimmon.

Cyprian of Carthage, (1977) 'Letter to Donatus'. In A. Field *From Darkness to Light*. Ann Arbor, Michigan: Servant Books.

Cyril of Jerusalem, (1977) 'Catechetical Lectures'. In A. Field *From Darkness to Light*. Ann Arbor, Michigan: Servant Books.

De Waal, E. (1988) *The Celtic Vision*. London: Darton, Longman and Todd.

Dearmer, P., Vaughan Williams, R. and Shaw, M. (eds.)(1928) *Oxford Book of Carols*. London: Oxford University Press.

Diószegi, V. (1968) *Trancing Shamans in Siberia*, in V. Diószegi *Popular Beliefs and Folklore Tradition in Siberia*. The Hague: Oosterhout.

Diószegi, V. (1983) 'Shamanism'. *Encyclopedia Britannica*, vol. 16, 15th Edition. Chicago: Helen Hemingway Benton.

Doyle, L. (transl.)(1948) *St. Benedict's Rule for Monastries*. Collegeville, Minnesota: The Liturgical Press.

Eder, M. (1958) 'Schamanismus in Japan'. *Paideuma* 4/7.

Eliade, M. (1957) *The Sacred and the Profane*. New York: Harvest Books, Harcourt, Brace and World.

Galili, E., Kaufman, D., and Weinstein-Evron, M. (1988) '8000 Years Under the Sea'. *Archaeology* 41, 66–67.

Green, M.A. (1983) *Festive Crafts*. London: Frederick Muller.

Guzie, T. (1981) *The Book of Sacramental Basics*. New York: Paulist Press.

Hall, J. (1974) *Subjects and Symbols in Art*. London: John Murray.

Harding, E. (1971) *Woman's Mysteries*. London: Rider.

Hausherr, I. (1982) *Penthos*. Kalamazoo, Michigan: Cistercian Publications.

Haynes, R. (1990) 'On with the Dance of Man and Beast'. *Catholic Herald*, 6th July.

Hindley, G. (ed.)(1981) *Larousse Encyclopedia of Music*. London: Hamlyn.

Holbrook, D. and Poston, E. (eds)(1967) *The Cambridge Hymnal*. Words anon., collection of Joshua Smith, New Hampshire. Cambridge: Cambridge University Press.

Hole, C. (1976) *A Dictionary of British Folk Customs*. London: Hutchinson.

Huxley, J. (1973) *Memories* Vol.2. London: George Allen and Unwin.

Jacobi, J. (1964) 'Symbols in an Individual Analysis'. In C. Jung (ed.) *Man and his Symbols*. London: Aldus Books.

Jaffé, A. (1964) 'Symbolism in the Visual Arts'. In C. Jung (ed.) *Man and his Symbols*. London: Aldus Books.

The Jerusalem Bible (1966) ed. Alexander Jones. London: Darton, Longman and Todd.

Jesu Corona Virginum, vespers hymn for feasts of virgins (1947) in *Liber Usualis* E. Rees (trans.). Rome: Desclée.

Julian of Norwich (1966) *Revelations of Divine Love*. C. Wolters. (trans.) Harmondsworth, Middlesex: Penguin.

Jungmann, J. (1960) *The Early Liturgy*. London: Darton, Longman and Todd.

Kalweit, H. (1988) *Dreamtime and Inner Space: the World of the Shaman*. London: Shambala.

Kleist, J. (trans.)(1946) *The Epistles of St. Clement of Rome and St. Ignatius of Antioch*. London: Longmans, Green & Co.

Knutsson, K.E. (1967) 'Authority and Change: a Study of the Kallu Institution among the Macha Galla of Ethiopia'. Göteborg, Sweden.

Lambeth, M. (1974) *Discovering Corn Dollies*. Aylesbury, Bucks: Shire Publications.

Leggat, P.O. and Leggat D.V. (1987) *The Healing Wells: Cornish Cults and Customs*. Redruth, Cornwall: Dyllansow Truran.

Lewis, I.M. (1971) *Ecstatic Religion—an Anthropological Study of Spirit Possession and Shamanism*. Harmondsworth, Middlesex: Penguin.

Long, A. (1976) *Praise Him in the Dance*. London: Hodder and Stoughton.

Mace, T. (1966) 'Musick's Monument', facsimile, collection *Le Choeur des Muses*. Paris: Édition de Centre National de la Recherche Scientifique.

Masson, G. (1965) *The Companion Guide to Rome*. London: Collins.

McCarthy, F. (1957) *Australia's Aborigines: their Life and Culture*. Melbourne, Australia: Colorgravure Publications.

Métraux, A. (1959) *Voodoo in Haiti* . H. Charteris (trans.). London: André Deutsch.

Moots, G. (1984) *Christian Iconography* unpublished essays. Albuquerque, New Mexico.

Moréchand, G. (1968) 'Le Chamanisme des Hmongs'. *Bulletin de l'Ecole Française de l'Extrême-orient*.

Murphy, G. (ed.)(1956) *Early English Lyrics, 8th–12th century*. Oxford University Press.

The New International Version Study Bible (1987) ed. Edwin Palmer. London: Hodder and Stoughton.

Nocent, A. (1977) *The Liturgical Year: Advent, Christmas, Epiphany*. Collegeville, Minnesota: The Liturgical Press.

Puthanangady, P. *Initiation to Christian Worship*. St. Peter's Seminary, India: Theological Publications in India.

Rahner, H. (1963 (i)) *Greek Myths and Christian Mystery*. B. Battershaw (trans.). London: Burns and Oates.

Rahner, H. (1963 (ii)) *Man at Play*. B. Battershaw and E. Quinn (trans.). London: Burns and Oates.

Rasmussen, K. (1927) 'Across Arctic America'. *Report of the Fifth Thule Expedition 1921–24*. New York.

Rasmussen, K. (1930) 'Intellectual Culture of the Igulik Eskimos'. *Report of the Fifth Thule Expedition, 1921–24* Vol.7, no.1. Copenhagen.

Rasmussen, K. (1931) 'Orpingalik, a Netsilingmint Eskimo'. *Report of the Fifth Thule Expedition, 1921–24'* vol.8. Copenhagen.

Rasmussen, K. (1929/1930) *The Intellectual Culture of the Igulik Eskimos*. Copenhagen.

Reclus, E. (art.)(1910–11) 'Fire' in *Encyclopedia Britannica*, vol.X, 11th Edition. Chicago: William Benton.

Rees, M. (1990) unpublished research. Coventry.

Rendell, J. (1976) *Your Book of Corn Dollies*. London: Faber and Faber.

Rhodes James, M. (trans.)(1924) 'Acts of Andrew' in *The Apocryphal New Testament*. Oxford: Clarendon Press.

Rolle, R. (1972) *The Fire of Love (1343)* C. Wolters (ed.).

Schreiter, R. (1988) *In Water and in Blood*. New York: Crossroad.

Smith, G. (1873–81) 'Eleventh Tablet of Izdubar Legend'. *Records of the Past VII*. London.

St. Augustine of Hippo (1930) *Select Letters*. Trans. J. Houston Baxter. London: William Heinemann.

Strunk, O. (1981 (i)) '*Source readings in Music History* selected and annotated by O. Strunk. Vol 1. *Antiquity and the Middle Ages*. London: Faber.

Strunk, O. (1981 (ii)) '*Source readings in music history*' selected and annotated by O. Strunk. Vol. 2. *The Renaissance* London: Faber.

Symeon the New Theologian, St. (1975) *Hymns of Divine Love*. G. Maloney (trans). Dimension Books: Denville, New Jersey.

Tugwell, S. (trans.)(1978) *The Nine Ways of Prayer of St. Dominic*. Dublin: Dominican Publications.

van der Kleij, G. (1991) unpublished lecture: Turvey Abbey.

Vince, J. (1969) *Discovering Saints in Britain*. Aylesbury, Bucks: Shire Publications.

Warner, R, (ed.)(1970) *Encyclopedia of World Mythology*. London: Peerage.

Weiler, E. (1980) *Jesus: A Pictorial History of the New Testament*. New York: Seabury Press.

Weiser, F. (1952) *The Christmas Book*. New York: Harcourt Brace.

Winstone, H. (ed.)(1975) *The Sunday Missal*. London: Collins.

Women's Institute Home Skills Publication (1979) *Corn Dollies from the Start*. London: Bell and Sons.

Wosien, M. (1974) *Sacred Dance: Encounter with the Gods*. London: Thames and Hudson.

Wulstan, D. (1968) unpublished lectures: Oxford University.

Young, B. (1991) *The Villein's Bible*. London: Barrie and Jenkins.

Index

Storymaking in Bereavement
Dragons Fight in the Meadow
Alida Gersie
ISBN 1 85302 176 8 320pp pb
ISBN 1 85302 065 6 hb
'This book is beautifully written... It is immensely rich
in its use of story, metaphor and literary allusion to
illustrate the process of grief and healing... I found this
book personally moving and deeply compassionate. In
addition to its overt theme, a book which touches its
reader so deeply provides a subtle lesson in how a
counsellor may allow herself to be deeply touched by
her client.'

– Counselling

'some very sensitive writing...a rich collection of stories
and workshops...it opens up feelings and thought
which...broaden the reader's own experience'

– Church Times

Alida Gersie is courseleader of the Postgraduate
Diploma (CNAA) in Dramatherapy at the Hertfordshire
College of Art & Design and is internationally known
for her work on storymaking.

Dramatherapy with Families, Groups and Individuals
Waiting in the Wings
Sue Jennings
ISBN 1 85302 014 1 160 pp illus hb
ISBN 1 85302 144 X pb
'Not only is it extremely well written, but the theoretical
models and issues outlined are worked through with
the use of detailed and clear examples... deserves to be
widely read by specialists and non-specialists alike...'

Counselling

Jessica Kingsley Publishers
116 Pentonville Road, London N1 9JB

Drama and Healing
The Roots of Drama Therapy
Roger Grainger
ISBN 1 85302 048 6 156 pp hb
The author shows how dramatherapy draws on both drama and ritual. He argues that personal construct theory provides a hermeneutically useful approach to the study of dramatherapy. He shows that dramatherapy itself is an effective treatment for depression and schizophrenia, having a measurable effect on thought disorder. Above all, the author is concerned not only to think rationally about dramatherapy, but to examine the specific relationship between rational thought and artistic experience which allows the second to act as the mediator of the first.

A Handbook of Enquiry in the Arts Therapies
One River Many Currents
Edited by Helen Payne
Foreword by John Rowan, Co-Director Serpent Institute
ISBN 1 85302 153 9 250pp pb
Exploring the relationship between research and practice in the arts therapies, this book examines the effects and processes of arts therapies interventions in health, education, community and social services settings, highlighting the urgent need for research to be undertaken and communicated to policy makers in order for it to have an effect on practice.
Helen Payne lectures in dance movement therapy in the Department of Art and Psychology, Hertfordshire College of Art and Design.

Jessica Kingsley Publishers
116 Pentonville Road, London N1 9JB

The Metaphoric Body
A Guide to Expressive Therapy through Images and Archetypes
Lea Barthal and Nira Ne'eman

ISBN 1 85302 152 O 224 pages pb

The Metaphoric Body is a guidebook and resource
offering suggestions, ideas, exercises and a way of
working towards the therapeutic process. The authors
show how the exploration of the body through
archetypal symbols transforms and facilitates change in
people's lives. As international pioneers with 35 years'
experience in the fields of movement, dance, dance
therapy, drama and art, the authors emphasise a holistic
approach which goes beyond the purely cognitive and
verbal.

Based on increasing understanding and awareness of
the body through movement improvisation and
exercises, the workshops incorporate exercises using
improvised drama, mask work, visual arts and written
work. Later workshops go on to extend the movement
into interaction with objects, the environment and other
people, and draw on images and symbols from the Old
Testament, Greek mythology and the Taoist Five
Elements.

Lea Barthal has taught extensively in the UK for 20
years, including posts with the Welsh College of Music
and Drama, East 15 Acting School, the School of Theatre
at Manchester Polytechnic and the Rose Bruford
College of Speech and Drama. She currently teaches
T'ai Chi Ch'uan and has a private counselling practice.
Nira Ne'eman is currently the Head of Department of
Movement and Dance, and Head of Department of
Integrated Arts in Education at the Oranium School of
Education of the Kibbutz Movement at the University
of Haifa. She also teaches Dance Therapy, Creative
Process and T'ai Chi Ch'uan at the 'Menashe' Regional
Dance Centre.

Jessica Kingsley Publishers
116 Pentonville Road, London N1 9JB

Symbols of the Soul
Therapy and Guidance Through Fairy Tales
Birgitte Brun, Ernst W. Pedersen
and Marianne Runberg
Foreword by Murray Cox
192 pages, illus ISBN 1 85302 107 5 hb
Fairy tales are part of our culture and history. They
have been with many of us since we were children.
During the last 20 years there has been an increasing
interest in psychoanalytically-oriented interpretations
of fairy tales. The authors show that fairy tales can be
used in therapy and guidance in a number of ways and
on many different levels. Using such stories in their
daily work proved beneficial for staff-members and
patients alike, generating a response of interest,
attention and sensitivity, underlining their point that
fairy tales have an impact on, and importance for,
everyone. A chapter is included on symbols in fairy
tales, which looks at why many sybols illustrate the
same phonomenon, but elicit different reactions from
individuals.
Birgitte Brun and **Marianne Runberg** are clinical psy-
chologists working in the Sct. Hans Hospital in Ros-
kilde, Denmark. **Ernst W. Pedersen** is the hospital
chaplain.

Music Therapy in Health and Education
Margaret Heal and Tony Wigram
ISBN 1 85302 175 X pb

Introduction to Dramatherapy
Sue Jennings
1 85302 115 6 pb

Jessica Kingsley Publishers
116 Pentonville Road, London N1 9JB

Storymaking in Education and Therapy

Alida Gersie and Nancy King

ISBN 1 85302 520 8 pb
ISBN 1 85302 519 4 hb

'The book is not only an invaluable resource, it also offers the reader many hours of delight, and more than delight, inspiration. It is a true discovery.'

– Dr Ofra Ayalon, Haifa University

'This is a lovely book...buy it'

– Nursing Times

'For the dramatherapist this book contains a rich variety of thought-provoking and inspiring material...a core text for dramatherapists to acquire'

– Dramatherapy

Play Therapy with Abused Children

Ann Cattanach

ISBN 1 85302 120 2 160pp hb

Ann Cattanach explores the uses of play therapy with abused children as a means of helping them to heal their distress and make sense of their experiences through expanding their own creativity in play. Ways of starting play therapy with abused children are described together with models of intervention which meet the particular needs of the child and the work-setting of the therapist; for example, short and medium term interventions, individual/group and sibling work.

Case histories of children who have experienced physical, emotional and sexual abuse are included, showing how play therapy was used to help them come to terms with past and prepare for the future.

Ann Cattanach MSc, CSTD, DTh lectures at the Institute of Dramatherapy and the Roehampton Institute. She is a therapist at the Harrow Health Authority Child and Family Service.

Jessica Kingsley Publishers
116 Pentonville Road, London N1 9JB

Art Therapy and Dramatherapy

Masks of the Soul
Sue Jennings and Åse Minde
1992 224 pages, illus ISBN 1 85302 027 hb
Based on more than ten years of research and practice
of art therapy and dramatherapy, in training, clinical
practice and theory, this book is the first to explore the
relationship and differences between art therapy and
dramatherapy. The first part of the book explores the
theoretical background and the history and practice of
the two therapies. The second part describes five major
themes that have been developed conjointly, making
use of dominant symbols and mythology. It outlines
actual method and practice.
Sue Jennings, PhD, is a Consultant Dramatherapist and
Teaching Fellow, and innovator of Dramatherapy and
Symbolic Play methods, currently working with abused
familes and infertility. **Ase Minde**, Dip ATh, is
Founder/Director of Art Therapy training in Norway.

Art Therapy in Practice

Edited by Marian Liebmann
1990 192 pages, 58 illus ISBN 1 85302 057 5 hb £24.50
ISBN 1 85302 058 3 pb £11.95
'This book offer(s) a valuable contribution to the
dissemination of information about the practice of art
therapy...fascinating reading.'
– Counselling Psychology Quarterly

Jessica Kingsley Publishers
116 Pentonville Road, London N1 9JB

Dramatherapy and Post Traumatic Stress Disorder
The Use of Dramatherapy in Its Treatment and Risk-Reduction
Linda Winn

ISBN 1 85302 183 X pb

CONTENTS 1.What is post traumatic stress disorder? Who can be affected? 2. The importance of normalisation in preventing breakdown. 3. Training and preparation in the reduction of risk of PTSD. 4. Debriefing i) Those involved in incident, ii) the debriefers. 5. Key concepts in the Treatment of PTSD. 6. The use of dramatherapy groups in the treatment of PTSD. 7. The use of dramatherapy in the treatment of individuals suffering from PTSD. Appendices. Index.

Focus on Psychodrama
The Therapeutic Aspects of Psychodrama
Peter Felix Kellermann
Foreword by Jonathan D Moreno

ISBN 1 85302 127 X pb

The author provides a comprehensive overview of the theory and practice of psychodrama, presenting a systematic analysis of its essential therapeutic ingredients. He specifies the core issues involved, discussing the interpersonal, the emotional, the imaginary, the behavioural and the cognitive elements. The book examines the professional roles assumed by psychodramatists and establishes the skills required in each role. Explored is the use of the concept of acting out, both in psychodrama and psychoanalysis, and the author also discusses the problem of resistance, and the importance of the concept and technique of closure in each psychodrama. A processing checklist is added at the end of the book as a systematic aid in evaluating the professional skills of the psychodramatist.

Jessica Kingsley Publishers
116 Pentonville Road, London N1 9JB

Movement and Drama in Therapy *2nd edition*
Audrey G. Wethered
128 pages ISBN 1 85302 199 7 pb
This classic book explores the role of drama, movement
and music in helping mentally disturbed patients to
emerge from their twilight world into a state where
they can begin to come to terms with themselves and
with daily living. The basic principles of movement are
outlined, and their use and practical value discussed.
The book is for those experienced in therapy, who
desire to understand movement, for those trained in
movement, who seek to apply what they have learned
in the therapeutic and other remedial ways, and as an
introduction to both movement and therapy for those in
other disciplines.
Audrey Wethered is one of the few people still living
who studied individually with Rudolf Laban. She has
put his theory and approach into practice in her work.
Now over 80 years old, she still works in the healing
field and teaches students.

Jessica Kingsley Publishers
116 Pentonville Road, London N1 9JB

DATE DUE

APR 1 8 2000		
DEC 1 3 2000		
8106101		
1-17-02		
3/12/03		
DEC 0 4 2008		
MAR 0 5 2009		
APR 0 2 2011		

GAYLORD   PRINTED IN U.S.A.